The Banality of Evil

The Banality of Evil

Hannah Arendt and "The Final Solution"

BERNARD J. BERGEN

ROWMAN & LITTLEFIELD PUBLISHERS, INC.
Lanham • Boulder • New York • Oxford

ROWMAN & LITTLEFIELD PUBLISHERS, INC.

Published in the United States of America
by Rowman & Littlefield Publishers, Inc.
4720 Boston Way, Lanham, Maryland 20706

12 Hid's Copse Road
Cumnor Hill, Oxford OX2 9JJ, England

British Library Cataloguing in Publication Information Available

Library of Congress Cataloging-in-Publication Data

Bergen, Bernard J.
    The banality of evil : Hannah Arendt and "the final solution" /
Bernard J. Bergen.
        p.   cm.
    Includes bibliographical references and index.
    ISBN 0-8476-9209-4 (alk. paper). — ISBN 0-8476-9210-8 (pbk.: alk.
paper)
        1. Arendt, Hannah—Views on the Holocaust.   2. Holocaust, Jewish
(1939–1945)—Causes.   3. Arendt, Hannah. Eichmann in Jerusalem.
I. Title.
D804.3.B463   1998
940.53′18—dc21   98-4044
                                                                     CIP

Printed in the United States of America

⊗™ The paper used in this publication meets the minimum requirements of
       American National Standard for Information Sciences—Permanence of
Paper for Printed Library Materials, ANSI Z39.48–1984.

This book is for my two fathers, Solomon and Eugene, who asserted themselves as individuals despite knowing full well how little they amounted to in that fabled "grand scheme of things."

Contents

Preface

The first book I read by Hannah Arendt was *Eichmann in Jerusalem.* Before I read it in 1963, all I knew about her was that she was a Jewish political scientist of some prominence who had escaped Nazi Germany and emigrated eventually to the United States. Her book, subtitled *A Report on the Banality of Evil,* had been previously serialized in the *New Yorker* and was provoking a firestorm of argument and conflict on the talk and party circuit that was obligatory for those, like me, who were just beginning an academic career. These were just skirmishes in what was becoming a mean war fought through book reviews, letters to the editor, and essays and articles in various newspapers, journals, and magazines, as well as in tumultuous public meetings.[1] It was an unforgiving war because it was being fought over the right to define what Arendt meant by associating the words *banal* and *evil* in the context of the most massive moral failure of the century: what the Nazis had called "the final solution of the problem of the Jews."

Ironically, what very few, if any, of the combatants on either side recognized at that time was that while Arendt, like everybody, defined the Final Solution as a massive moral failure, this was only the obvious starting point for defining *the banality of evil* in very different terms. The war was serious, and while everybody was certain of the righteousness of their cause, very few, I am convinced, including myself, actually knew what the war was truly about.

At the time there were two ways of reading *Eichmann in Jerusalem* that functioned like flags rallying both Jews and non-Jews to opposing armies. The army that I eagerly joined read *the banality of evil* as telling us that we are all Eichmanns—that is, there is an Eichmann in each of us waiting only for the correct sociohistorical conditions to be released. We knew, with the certainty that makes good soldiers and without bothering to question what Arendt wanted us to know, that her phrase *the*

ix

banality of evil signified the need for a moral mission to prevent the repetition of genocidal murder by shaping the world's political systems in our time to both allow for and protect individual rights and freedoms. In other words, we read the egregious moral failure of the Final Solution as calling us to discover the causal laws that govern the forms that humans give to the social institutions that govern them. It did not really matter whether we knew or not the extent to which Arendt shunned being called a "political scientist." As a Jewish refugee from Nazi tyranny, could she have been anything but a partisan for the human sciences, knowing that *prevention* was a word that naturally followed *causality* and *prediction?*

The opposition, on the other hand, regarded our interpretation of *the banality of evil* as a three-pronged, egregious insult to the Jewish victims of the Nazi genocide. In the first place, went the argument, grounding an understanding of the Final Solution in abstract, universal, sociohistorical laws that presumably govern the form and function of the societies in which all humans must live means viewing the Jews themselves as having been an integral part of European societies that had never treated them as anything but hated outsiders from the beginning of the history of the Jewish Diaspora in Europe. In the second place (and related to this), to read into the meaning of the Final Solution a call to search for its causes means to willfully look away from what was plain for all to see: that the Nazi murder of the Jews was an event in Jewish history in which Gentiles throughout the world were, at best, observers secretly deriving pleasure from a pornography of death, or, at worst, Germans bringing to a culmination the long history of European anti-Semitism. And in the third place, related to this, to associate the word *banal* with the Nazi genocide against the Jews dissipates its singular horrors by merging them into the stream of commonplace horrors that marks the movement of human history. To add injury to this insult, associating the singular horrors of the Nazi genocide with other murderous events in history is an open invitation to formulate causes that can only amount to mitigation of the guilt of the Nazis for their atrocities. This, in fact, actually proved to be the case in later years.[2]

The war, however, between these opposed readings of the meaning of *the banality of evil* was truly being fought by armies that were clashing in the dark of night. Everybody involved seemed blind to recognizing that for Arendt, defining the meaning of the Final Solution as a massive moral failure is to state the obvious, which, as is almost always the case, misses the meaning of things. In retrospect, I find that this blindness was unremarkable because both the small skirmishes I was involved in and the major battles fought through the media were almost always conducted on the ground of the one text, *Eichmann in Jerusalem,* which hardly dealt at all with what every combative argument eventually boiled down to: the origins of totalitarianism and the human condition. *Eichmann in Jerusalem* was designed to be a very thin book, a "report" that would contain little, if any, dense conceptual material about either subject. Arendt had already published two books, which carried her reputation at that time, with the titles of those subjects (*The Origins of Totalitarianism* and *The Human Condition*). *Eichmann in Jerusalem* could be read as an isolated report, but it was actually part of a continuously unfolding body of work that would never be finished until Arendt's death.

What was remarkable, in retrospect, was Arendt's naive belief that her report would not provoke a heated battle in which both sides would ignore those books. The phrase *the banality of evil* was too provocative, too inflammatory to allow reading *Eichmann in Jerusalem* as part of a continuing work-in-progress. It would have meant not fighting over its meaning but affirming rather Arendt's admission, made at least twice in her work,[3] that she herself was not sure of its meaning when she first used it because its meaning could only emerge from her work-in-progress that, like all other works-in-progress, is a continuous struggle to articulate its own meaning. It would not be amiss to say that the ultimate trope in this regard was provided by Freud when he likened his own work to an archaeological dig. For Arendt, calling Eichmann the "banality of evil" was part of her "dig."

True, I would be ingenuous to a fault to argue that Arendt went to Jerusalem solely to further disclose to herself the meaning of her collective work. She no doubt had other agendas of which she herself was probably not fully aware. But these are beside the point. They were certainly not, as so many said outright, to side with the Nazis against the Jews. The point that is important here is that both sides that were fighting the war instigated by the appearance of *Eichmann in Jerusalem* saw no need to read her work that preceded and grounded it. Perhaps we did not want to read her work because it would have prepared us to follow her thinking about the problem that Eichmann represented in a direction that would have subverted the call to arms of both warring parties.

Arendt went to Jerusalem prepared by her previous work to define Eichmann as a problem who could not be made to go away with rhetorical magic. No preconceptions—legal, scientific, or otherwise—could substitute for listening to him as he literally appeared to her in that courtroom: As a person who was conveying the meaning of his experiences to others by speaking about himself. But during his long cross-examination and even before, when he spoke to his interrogators in the pretrial examination, Eichmann spoke about himself as if no time at all had passed since he had been the SS officer responsible for shipping millions of Jews to their deaths. There was nothing that Eichmann said about himself, during or leading up to that long trial, that he would not have said about himself when he was vested with the power of the Nazi SS.

It was not until many years after the battle over Arendt's book had receded—the war never really ended: it just subsided—when I was motivated to read everything Arendt wrote because I was going to use her work in a course on totalitarianism I was to teach that I realized how my indifference to this fact about Eichmann had blinded me to what the war had really been about. That Eichmann had nothing new to say about himself fifteen years after the horrendous crimes he had committed seemed totally unremarkable to me and, as I see it now, to almost everyone else who fought on either side. It signaled that being an SS officer, with all that that entailed both behaviorally and psychologically, had been his *identity:* the concept that, in our time, has come to anchor both the possibilities and the limits of the self. It continues to be the concept—I think *trope* would label it more accurately[4]—that solves, for our time, the problem presented by the discovery of the power of the self born with the origin of modernity. For how could we create modern political systems on the basis of rights, obligations, and duties that accrue to individuals unless individuals think of themselves as having a persistent identity that is continuous through time? For my side, Eichmann's identity had been anchored to his role as an SS officer by the powerful forces of society that shaped his entire development as a self. It was just a question of knowing the details of how those perverse causal forces played on him. For the other side, his identity was anchored to the poisonous forces of anti-Semitism, whose toxic effect on him was manifest in every detail of the grotesque extermination program of the Jews in which he played a key role. We had been fighting a war, in effect, over who had the proprietary rights to that trope *identity,* which we took to be the referent for Arendt's phrase *the banality of evil.*

It was precisely the power of this trope *identity* that blinded us to the direction that Arendt was taking toward the meaning of the term. That Eichmann on trial in Jerusalem was unable to say anything new about himself was indeed his way of telling us about his unchanging identity. But Arendt came to Jerusalem prepared by her previous work to refuse to use *identity* as a concept that exhaustively accounts for what one hears when others speak about their experiences. With this refusal she was reversing the modern formula that we combatants were apparently unable to reverse: Identity is not the end point but the starting point for understanding the meaning of what somebody is saying about who they are. To treat identity as the end point would have been to dissolve the concrete form of Eichmann by which he was experienced by everyone who saw and heard him as an individual speaking about himself into an object shaped by causal forces, social or attitudinal. By refusing to compromise her way of experiencing Eichmann's appearance, Arendt put into relief a different and unforeseen direction for establishing the meaning of *the banality of evil* barely visible in that thin book *Eichmann in Jerusalem* but nevertheless clearly stated: an inability to think.

Arendt tells us throughout her work that regarding totalitarianism, what is unprecedented cannot be measured by the tradition of thought in the so-called human sciences, which treat their concepts as if they referred to causal forces that determine the experiences of humans and the shape of the world they build. In *The Human Condition* Arendt tells us what her work is all about: "[N]othing more than to think what we are doing."[5] This is worthy of being read as an epigraph for her entire body of work, especially if we were to amend it to read: "To think what we are doing by thinking over from the very beginning everything we ever thought we were doing." What must be thought through from the beginning about the meaning of the Final Solution is something far more radical than its meaning as a moral failure: the very idea of the individual. *The banality of evil* does not refer to the Final Solution as just one more commonplace evil in human history, but to an unprecedented evil that arose from the commonplace in the sense of "the ordinary." And there is nothing that can strike us as more ordinary than the existence of human individuals who speak to each other constantly about their experiences.

From the moment when the idea of the individual became significant—and who can say exactly when that historical moment was except that we have mythologized it as the very origin of our modernity—the sign of being an individual has been thought of as being an experiencing being who conveys the meaning of his experiences to himself and to others. But the Final Solution forces us to think about the authority that meaning can wield over experience.

Arendt said she wanted to go to Jerusalem to see Eichmann, but she was surely not naive enough to believe that she would see someone whose appearance would be monstrous. In fact, what she brought with her to Jerusalem was an unfolding work that prepared her to hear something monstrous that no one else heard, at least in that courtroom: Eichmann represented a line that had been crossed by virtually an entire nation into a region where meaning assumed total authority over experience—erasing experience itself as the sign for experiencing beings that they were individuals.

In describing Eichmann as *the banality of evil,* Arendt had invented a phrase whose foundation she had already laid in terms of the fragility of individuals thinking of themselves as individuals simply because they speak about their experience of the meaning of things. The full meaning of this fragility would preoccupy her in the years following her Eichmann book until she came to grips with it in her final book, left incomplete by her death, *The Life of the Mind.* Arendt, who had the temerity to make a virtue of the term *pariah,* would see at the beginning of her work that it is the experience of being an individual that insulates us from committing great evils like the Final Solution, and, by the end of her work, would define that experience in radically unique terms.

To read Arendt is to allow ourselves to be stripped of the armor of our preconceptions that deflects reading anything whose meaning does not work to predict a future that always seems to slip out of our control. To grasp the meaning of the Final Solution is to grasp it as a call to think through from the beginning our most treasured belief: That we speak as individuals when we give an account of what we are doing. What Arendt saw clearly from the beginning to the end of her work is that we will never understand the Final Solution in terms of the abstractions of political and moral theory, but only in terms of what it means to think, will, and judge; to use the life of the mind that, when it is moribund, defines a line that was once crossed into a region in which terror becomes a normal feature of the world. It is in Arendt's work that we find the immense significance of the Final Solution pointing to where we can locate that line: in the fragile banalities of who we think we are and what we think we are doing.

∼   ∼

Arendt's work confronts a broad spectrum of traditional concepts central to the canonical literature of modern political philosophy and the human sciences. Reading her work calls for a binocular focus on the new meanings she gives to old, reliable words such as *freedom, action, identity, society, politics, anti-Semitism, causality,* and many more. As a result, her work has given rise to what Scott and Stark have called "an academic cottage industry"[6] that has produced a substantial number of in-depth studies of the way her concepts articulate with one or more traditional meanings. This book, however, is not one of them. My binocular reading has been on the Final Solution and the direction her work takes toward its meaning. This is not along a road straight as an arrow and clearly marked like those highways in our Western states that are always startling to an Easterner like myself. Her work meanders considerably, but I have tried to mark its direction by organizing it around four interlocking problems that I feel are crucial to reading it as a continuous journey toward understanding the Final Solution as *the banality of evil:* the problem of the Final Solution, the problem of thinking, the problem of "The Political," and the problem of terror.

Finally, I should point out the spirit in which I hope this book will be read. There is one way in which I do not follow Arendt: while she used the definite article in the title of her books, I do not offer in this book *the* reading of Arendt's work, but only *a* reading of it.

Notes

1. Those who think I am exaggerating when I call what was going on a "mean war" should consult the chapter "Curia Posterior: Eichmann in Jerusalem" in Elisabeth Young-Bruehl's *Hannah Arendt: For Love of the World* (New Haven, CT: Yale University Press, 1982), esp. 347–49.

2. See Perry Anderson, "On Emplotment: Two Kinds of Ruin," in *Probing the Limits of Representation: Nazism and the Final Solution,* ed. Saul Friedlander (Cambridge, MA: Harvard University Press, 1992), 54.

3. Once in an exchange of letters with Scholem shortly after publication of *Eichmann in Jerusalem,* and once in her last work, published posthumously, *The Life of the Mind.* See "An Exchange of Letters Between Gershom Scholem and Hannah Arendt," *Encounter* (January 1964): 51–56; and Hannah Arendt, "Introduction" in *The Life of the Mind* (New York: Harcourt, Brace, Jovanovitch, 1978), 3.

4. *Identity* as a concept is meant to represent the self as a system of unified components such as drives, desires, traits, memories, self-images, etc. But as Roger Brown has confessed in his textbook on social psychology, "Identity is a concept no one has defined with precision, but it seems we can move ahead anyway, because everyone roughly understands what is meant." Quoted in William Ray Arney, *Thoughts Out of School* (in press).

5. Hannah Arendt, *The Human Condition* (Chicago: University of Chicago Press, 1958), 5.

6. Joanna Vecchiarelli Scott and Judith Chelius Stark, eds., "Introduction: 'New Beginnings'," in *Love and Saint Augustine by Hannah Arendt* (Chicago: University of Chicago Press, 1996), 125.

Acknowledgments

My thanks to Claudewell S. Thomas, M.D., for lighting a fire under the project during our visit to Auschwitz; Lou Renza, Ph.D., for his impeccable insights into structuring texts; George Patrick, M.D., for many hours of fruitful discussion about Arendt and her work; the late Professor Bernard Segal, Ph.D., for pressing me to think critically about totalitarianism; Daniel Krymkowski, Ph.D., for helping me think about Europe, Poland, and the Jews in new ways; and William Ray Arney, Ph.D., and Vera Bergen for critically reading the completed manuscript.

1

The Problem of "The Final Solution"

~ 1 ~

The problem of whether it is possible to grasp the meaning of what the Nazis called "the final solution of the problem of the Jews" comes into focus when we give credence to Appelby, Hunt, and Jacob's carefully argued conclusion that: "What historians do best is to make connections with the past to illuminate the problems of the present and the potential of the future."[1] What significance can we attribute to "The Final Solution" when the suffering of its victims overwhelms our ability to understand it? To what lessons can the suffering of the victims of the Final Solution point when we cannot even give what happened to them a name? "Holocaust" is misleading because it is a metaphor for the practice of sacrifice, and as Berel Lang points out: "[T]he Nazi genocide against the Jews had none of the properties of a sacrifice except for its design of willful destruction: no intentionality on the part of those sacrificed, no sense of loss or of giving by those 'offering' the sacrifice, no evocation of a good to be redeemed by the act itself."[2] Wiesel makes the same point in different terms when he states that in Auschwitz "[t]he executioner killed for nothing, the victim died for nothing. No God ordered one to prepare the stake, nor the other to mount it."[3] The name "Shoah" is also not apt, because as Lang further observes, while its designations of "'wasteland,' or 'destruction' (as in Isaiah 10:3 and Proverbs 3:25) . . . are more accurately descriptive than 'Holocaust' because they imply a breach or turning point in history . . . these references, too, have theological, or at least mediating overtones."[4]

Every explanation of the Final Solution must confront the loyalty of virtually an entire nation to a regime that made its invention and

1

operation of a "killing machine"[5] possible. Explanations seem to fall short of conveying the horrific suffering it produced. We seem destined to respond to the Final Solution as a radical evil that, because it cannot be understood, leaves us either holding our breath in the hope that something like it will never happen again, or searching for signs that it might be happening again so that we can intervene to stop it.

It is in relation to the judgment that the Final Solution was a radical evil that Arendt's work gains a certain significance. While her work, as it is so often read, certainly lends itself to being divided into different topics, it is also supplied with a unifying thread by its bearing on the meaning of the Final Solution. Her first great work, *The Origins of Totalitarianism,* can be said to be her starting point for a project to understand the Final Solution, and no body of work can ever be said to leave its starting point behind. Her last book, assembled and published posthumously, *The Life of the Mind,* was prompted in part, she tells us, "from my attending the Eichmann trial in Jerusalem. In my report of it I spoke of 'the banality of evil.' Behind that phrase, I held no thesis or doctrine, although I was simply aware of the fact that it went counter to our tradition of thought—literary, theological, or philosophic—about the phenomenon of evil."[6] Her book on the Eichmann trial, of course, followed *The Origins of Totalitarianism* and *The Human Condition,* the theses of which she brought with her to the trial in Jerusalem.

Arendt's book *The Origins of Totalitarianism,* despite the portentous "the" in its title, is a peculiar history. Early on reviewers in the professional journals judged the book as lacking a rigorous approach to theory formation and testing.[7] But Arendt, in a response to Eric Voegelin's review—the only response to reviews that she ever published—defines its peculiarity in other terms: "I failed to explain the particular method which I came to use, and to account for a rather unusual approach . . . to the whole field of political and historical sciences as such. One of the difficulties of the book is that it does not belong to any school and hardly uses any of the officially recognized or officially controversial instruments."[8] In other words, as far as Arendt is concerned, the peculiarity of the book does not lie in its being deficient in established methodology, but in failing to explicate a method that is at odds with established methods. There is no question that this is true, as far as it goes, but it does not go far enough. The peculiarity of *The Origins of Totalitarianism* does not lie in its use of an unorthodox methodology, which incidentally, despite confessing to its use, Arendt never explicates anywhere in her work, but in something more profound: its redefinition of the Final Solution as a problem to be understood.

Arendt's insistence on *The Origins of Totalitarianism* as a peculiar history cannot be taken lightly. While she agrees with Hunt, Appelby, and Jacobs on the task of the historian, the thrust of *The Origins of Totalitarianism* is to raise the question of whether we are missing the point by defining the Final Solution solely as the kind of event we must seek to prevent in our own time. This redefinition of the Final Solution as a problem to be understood appears at the beginning of her book in her unusual approach to the subject of totalitarianism itself. There have been two, and only two, totalitarian regimes in history, Arendt tells us: Nazi Germany and Stalinist Russia, both of which were characterized by a rule of terror and murder, and both were driven by different ideologies of national destiny. Moreover, both were "unprecedented" (to use her own term) in history.

Arendt in her reply to Voegelin's review uses the term "unprecedented" in the strongest sense: "What is unprecedented in totalitarianism is not primarily its ideological content, but the event of totalitarian domination itself." She is criticizing Voegelin for thinking that the essence of totalitarianism reveals itself in the form of its political thought shaped from the past: "Professor Voegelin seems to think that totalitarianism is only the other side of liberalism, positivism, and pragmatism. But whether one agrees with liberalism or not . . . the point is that liberals are clearly not totalitarians. This, of course, does not exclude the fact that liberal or positivistic elements lend themselves to totalitarian thinking; but such affinities would only mean that one has to draw even sharper distinctions because of the *fact* that liberals are not totalitarians."[9] The twentieth century is not marked by the ambiguities of political thinking, but by the brute fact of totalitarianism: "What is unprecedented in totalitarianism is not primarily its ideological content, but the *event* of totalitarian domination itself. This can be seen clearly if we have to admit that the deeds of its considered policies have exploded our traditional categories of political thought . . . and the standards of our moral judgement."[10]

The *fact* of totalitarianism as an unprecedented historical event is a constant throughout Arendt's work. As a discussant at a conference on totalitarianism in 1953 she criticizes Carl Friederich for missing the point by speaking about what he called totalitarianism's "peculiar moral obtuseness." "The point," Arendt states:

> Is not the use of violence per se, not even on an unprecedented scale, but that "totalitarian indifference" to moral considerations is actually based on a reversal of all our legal and moral concepts, which ultimately rest on the commandment, "Thou shalt not kill." Against this, totalitarian "morals" preaches almost openly the precept: Thou shalt kill! . . . In other words, the peculiarity of totalitarian crimes is that they are committed for different reasons and in a different framework which has a "morality" of its own. The morality is contained in the ideology, or rather what totalitarianism has made of the respective ideologies which it inherited from the past.[11]

The point Arendt is making is both subtle and profound. There is a reason and logic, however perverse, behind the terror and murder of totalitarian regimes that waits to be understood; but this reason and logic cannot be understood by simply assuming that they were inherited from ideologies that preceded the regime's advent to power. In other words, to be more specific, while the Final Solution is consonant with anti-Semitic ideologies that were never absent in Europe since the beginning of the Diaspora, the Final Solution represents the pursuit of a purpose that was not caused by and cannot be an effect of those anti-Semitic ideologies. She states this clearly in her 1967 preface to the revised edition of *The Origins of Totalitarianism*: "The only direct, unadulterated consequence of nineteenth century antisemitic movements was not Nazism, but on the contrary, Zionism, which, at least in its Western ideological form, was a kind of counterideology, the 'answer' to antisemitism."[12]

It is a startling statement. Arendt is radically divorcing the Final Solution from its meaning as the culmination of a history of European anti-Semitism. Her refusal of this meaning of the Final Solution had more than a startling effect when she made it the opening theme in her report on the Eichmann trial in Jerusalem. In her opening chapter, which she ironically entitled "The House of Justice" after the name of the newly constructed auditorium where the trial was taking place, she sarcastically observes that "this courtroom is not a bad place for the show trial David Ben-Gurion, prime minister of Israel, had in mind when he decided to have Eichmann kidnapped in Argentina and brought to the District Court of Jerusalem to stand trial for his role in the 'final solution of the Jewish question.'"[13] As Arendt perceived it, the only ones in the courtroom who wanted to put Eichmann on trial for what a trial in the name of justice must be about—Eichmann's actual deeds—were the judges, whom Arendt never fails to treat with respect and honor. Arendt herself, along with everyone else in the courtroom, from the beginning never questioned Eichmann's guilt. More to the point, for everyone in that courtroom except Arendt the meaning of the Final Solution was never in question.

For the Israelis, following Ben-Gurion, everything about the Final Solution had been settled: the Jewish question, the German question, and the places both occupy in the process of history that caused it. The purpose of the trial was to display the truth of what was always known. As Arendt states it, paraphrasing Ben-Gurion as well as using his own words:

> The Jews in the Diaspora were to remember how Judaism "four thousand years old, with its spiritual creations and its ethical strivings, its Messianic aspirations," had always faced "a hostile world," how the Jews had degenerated until they went to their death like sheep, and how only the establishment of a Jewish state had enabled Jews to hit back, as Israelis had done in the War of Independence, in the Suez adventure, and in the almost daily incidents on Israel's unhappy borders. And if the Jews outside Israel had to be shown the difference between Israeli heroism and Jewish submissive weakness, there was a lesson for those inside Israel too: "the generation of Israelis who have grown up since the holocaust" were in danger of losing their ties with the Jewish people and, by implication, with their own history. "It is necessary that our youth remember what happened to the Jewish people. We want them to know the most tragic facts in our history."[14]

One can hardly imagine carrying into that Jerusalem courtroom an attitude, in which one regards the meaning of the Final Solution as an open question, more calculated than Arendt's to wound the sensibilities of Jews everywhere, in Israel as well as in the modern Diaspora. Once a Zionist herself, Arendt had always approved of the Zionist intention to found a Jewish nation in Palestine. Zionism for Jews, she had written, was "not only a guide to reality, but reality itself; not simply a key to history, but the experience of history itself."[15] But as Kaplan has observed, if for Arendt Zionism's "intention was correct . . . its actualization [was] tragically limited and defective."[16] Arendt broke with the Zionist movement because she opposed "[t]he often asserted conviction that Zionism was the project 'of a people without a land for a land without a people.'"[17] This was not a basis for bringing Jews as a people into political life for the first time since the start of the Diaspora.

But for Jews, under the tutelage of the Zionists, the Nazi's Final Solution of the Jewish question finally solved the question of Jewish identity. In the latter part of the nineteenth century the historical situation faced by emancipated Jews was an anti-Semitism that had become grounded in racist ideology. The question of Jewish identity had reached a fork in the road: was this racist anti-Semitism redeemable or not? In either case Jews must do something, but what must they do? In the pitiless light of the Final Solution anyone could see that there were no longer any political questions whose answers could fragment Jewish identity. In fact, there had never really been such questions. Only the blindness of the Jews themselves to the remorseless power of Jew-hatred had allowed such questions to ever have been taken seriously. The indifference to the suffering of the Jews manifested at the Nuremberg trial, treating it as simply one more crime among other crimes committed by the Germans, would influence the trial in Jerusalem—a trial designed so that no Jew would ever again be able to question his or her identity as a Jew living in a world of non-Jews, whom he or she must forever suspect will be hostile. As Arendt puts it: "[I]n the words of Davar, the organ of Mr. Ben-Gurion's Mapai party: 'Let world opinion know this, that not only Nazi Germany was responsible for the destruction of six million Jews of Europe'. . ."; or, "in Ben-Gurion's own words, 'We want the nations of the world to know . . . and they should be ashamed.'"[18]

Arendt's bluntness in refusing Ben-Gurion's lesson about the Final Solution as the culmination of an unbroken history of Jew-hating in Europe—a naive bluntness in that she could have thought that arguing the refusal of this lesson at Eichmann's trial, no less, would not make her book vulnerable to being read as a misprision—was only the bluntness in sharp relief that had already been expressed in *The Origins of Totalitarianism:* Jewish history conceived as "an unbroken continuity of persecutions, expulsions, and massacres from the end of the Roman Empire to the Middle Ages, the modern era and down to our own time, frequently embellished by the idea that modern antisemitism is no more than a secularized version of popular medieval superstitions is no less fallacious (though of course less mischievous) than the corresponding anti-semitic notion of a Jewish secret society that has ruled, or aspired to rule, the world since antiquity."[19]

It had been, of course, this last anti-Semitic notion that the Nazis used to inflame and exacerbate German anti-Semitic attitudes, especially to facilitate the regime's rise to power. Nevertheless, Arendt's divorce of the meaning of the Final Solution from the anti-Semitism that preceded it in European history is a radical divorce because she takes one more step: "Regimes," Arendt insists, "become truly totalitarian only when they have left behind their revolutionary phase and the techniques needed for the seizure and consolidation of power—without, of course, ever abandoning them, should the need arise again."[20] What this implies is that even if we could imagine having the most comprehensive and complete knowledge of anti-Semitism throughout German history, we could not derive an explanation of the Final Solution from the Nazi exploitation of it. Arendt is taking the step of defining the vitriolic anti-Semitism of the Nazis that was instrumental in the mass murder of the Jews as different from the anti-Semitism that preceded it. The significance of this step highlights what it is that makes *The Origins of Totalitarianism* a peculiar history that departs from the "established fields of the political and historical sciences."

Peukert and Hobsbawm, in a general way, can be taken as representations of how those established fields approach the problem of understanding the Final Solution. It is clear to Peukert that: "[t]he history of the Jews during the Weimar Republic . . . cannot be viewed solely in the light of their terrible fate during the Third Reich. Anti-Semitic discrimination certainly existed, but the situation was a complex one. . . ."[21] One of the complexities to which Peukert is referring is that Jews entering the Weimar period were legatees of a process of becoming model bourgeois Germans that began early in the nineteenth century. As Kaplan points out, they had "not only internalized the economic and cultural standards of the bourgeoisie but also became ardent admirers and promoters of many of its values."[22] Craig affirms that: "[t]here was nothing more German than those Jewish businessmen, doctors, lawyers, and scholars who volunteered for war service as a matter of course in 1914."[23] They were not alien outsiders living in a strange land.

While, as Peukert observes: "[t]he establishment of the Weimar Republic completed the process of Jewish emancipation in Germany,"[24] as the assassination of Rathenau in 1923 testified, German anti-Semitism precluded Jews from ever being seen as true Germans, a part of the German volk, laying claim to ties with ancient German culture and the Germanic soul. However, anti-Semitic rhetoric, which was an integral part of the complicated turmoil of political conflict during the Weimar period, never had the force of the degrading rhetoric characterizing German Jews as subhuman pariahs that it assumed with the Nazis. It was the "Ostjude" who bore the brunt, as it had for decades in Germany, of pre-Nazi dehumanizing, anti-Semitic rhetoric. Peukert concludes that: "[T]he rise of antisemitic discrimination and the role of anti-Jewish racial hatred within National Socialist ideology were not the outcome of events within the history of the Jews in Germany, but are to be accounted for as part of the evolution of the German radical right."[25]

Hobsbawm agrees completely. He makes the distinction between what he calls "grass roots anti-Semitism," which took such diverse forms as "striking workers [who] were apt, even when members of non-racist labor movements, to attack Jewish shopkeepers, and to think of their employers as Jews . . ." and "political anti-Semitism" where "violence came by decree above, as in November 1938."[26]

Arendt would not dispute that the Nazis exploited German anti-Semitism to gain power. But she would not leave it at that because of the assumption that the unprecedented actions comprising the Final Solution can be accounted for by "politicized" anti-Semitic ideas from the past used by the Nazi regime to sustain and expand its political power. In other words she was refusing the assumption that the Final Solution must be understood, as far as it can be understood at all, in terms of a politically motivated act by a regime that, for one reason or another and in one way or another, ran amuck while trying to sustain and expand its power using an ideologically justified terror. Arendt states her disagreement categorically: "In order to fight totalitarianism, one need understand only one thing: Totalitarianism is the most radical denial of freedom. Yet this denial of freedom is common to all tyrannies and is of no primary importance for understanding the peculiar nature of totalitarianism."[27] The similarities between tyrannies and totalitarian regimes are superficial: "[B]oth concentrate all power in the hands of one man, who uses this power in such a way that he makes all other men absolutely and radically impotent."[28]

In effect, the tyrant would like to literally be Hobbes's Leviathan— like an apparition omnipresent in the conduct of everyday life. But the vision that fuels totalitarian regimes is not to dominate the conduct of everyday life but to break down "the whole structure of morality, the whole body of commands and prohibitions"[29] that makes what had been everyday life possible. This destruction of the continuity of tradition, of what can be carried from the past to make the past continuous with the anticipated future, is what Arendt points to when she states that: "[t]otal domination for totalitarian regimes is never an end in itself."[30] If we look for the end that the Nazis pursued in terms of the kind of nation they envisioned in the images they favored during the period of gaining and consolidating their power, in certain fundamental respects we would find nothing different in the double sense of untraditional and not shared than with other nations. Perhaps those widely distributed pictures, both stills and movies, of Hitler with German children say it all. Hitler is usually gazing at, patting on the cheek, or receiving flowers from children who conform to the ideal Aryan image and are usually wearing traditional garb. Hitler's face usually has a more natural, softer, avuncular look than we are used to seeing. One gets the feeling that he might be adoring as much as being adored. And why not? The children are the future of the Volkisch nation. The idea that the German nation had a special character is usually traced to the nineteenth-century historian Herder, with a conventional caveat to the effect that he was not a racist but a cultural relativist. His idea fused, however, with "a much older tradition of 'Teutomania'"[31] to endow the German national character with a relative superiority to all others, especially the French and English, who made rival claims.

While these three nations made competing claims to cultural superiority, they all had at least two things in common: the certainty that the Slavs were primitive barbarians, and the certainty that the certainty of their claims was supported by those amendments that translated Darwin's Theory of Evolution into Social Darwinism. This doctrine, which began to dominate nationalist thinking well before the Nazi movement offered all peoples a nationalist ideology in which a citizen could know himself, as Arendt puts it, "as though he were a falling stone, endowed with the gift of consciousness and therefore capable of observing, while he is falling, Newton's laws of gravitation."[32] It would have been more pertinent had Arendt troped that knowledge in terms of an upward-climbing movement, because it drew from the Darwinian idea that it is an evolutionary movement governed by the unchanging, timeless laws of nature that determine the nature of all living things. These laws reveal themselves in the way living things evolve, whose nature is the legatee of time.

Social Darwinism inserted into Darwin's Theory of Evolution the human preoccupation with creating a future that redeems human suffering from history. For Social Darwinists, this redemption is what human history is about because history expresses a progression toward transcending the barbarous struggles between human groups that have been drenched in blood and misery. Rationalists, moralists, and theologians may see a fatal contradiction in the argument that invariant laws of nature—the barbarous struggles that constitute the law of the survival of the fittest—can move toward transcending themselves through human history. But this objection because they do not understand that the Social Darwinist amendment to Darwin's Theory bonds the idea of progress to a sacred calling in a way that creates a myth. And myths, Ricouer notes, "speak of the beginning and end of evil. . . . Evil—defilement or sin—is the sensitive point . . . which myth makes explicit in its own way."[33]

The idea of progress took on mythic proportions when it signified the destiny nature assigns to one human group in order to transform human nature. If Darwin had demonstrated, in the service of his thesis on the continuity between animals and humans, how animals mimicked humans when birds sang, maternal beasts cared for their young, and the like, why couldn't there be humans who mimicked humans? Knowledge of the laws of evolution sorts out the questions of who among humans carries the destiny of the species, and who obstructs that destiny as the secret corruption that afflicts human history with its misery. The children photographed with Hitler signify the transparent measure of that racial purity that is threatened by secret corruption. And Hitler, in his uniform with its prominent Nazi armband, clearly signifies not just a protective force, but an achieving force demanded by the law of social evolution that is the struggle for survival—an old story, and in Social Darwinist terms, the oldest of stories.

But what was unique about Hitler's call to the German people to create a racially purified nation out of the secret corruption of the past was that it was not bombast—he meant it. To mean something is to be earnest about it, to create events by acting rather than merely thinking about events. Thinking may well be a form of action but by itself it only creates a space in which dreamers can dream their dreams. Being earnest is known by those in the West as the power that drove the scientific revolution that transformed the world. In a sense, Hitler's rise to power was yet another national revolution in a long history of European national revolutions, but it was not a political revolution. It was another revolution of earnestness in the West to change the world in an unprecedented way by using the fruits of the first revolution to do it.

~ **2** ~

From its beginning, the Nationalsozialistische Deutsche Arbeiterpartei (NSDAP) was Hitler's party; and from the beginning its political program *was* Hitler. Peukert states that: "After his release from Landsberg prison in December 1924, Hitler set about reorganizing his party with remarkable energy. . . . Ideologically speaking . . . the NSDAP stood for a melange of ideas and grievances that were far from original and indeed were common to much of the German right. . . ."[34] The center of gravity that held together the party's often contradictory *melange* of well-worn ideas was Hitler himself, whose own vision of the well-worn idea of a Volksgemeinschaft carried with it the sense that, all ideas aside, the NSDAP represented something new. Its pattern of recruitment made it clear that it did not represent the interests of any particular social class from which Germans had traditionally derived their personal and political identities. The party concentrated on recruiting relatively young members who, like Himmler for example, had never served in World War I, or who, like Hitler himself, had barely turned forty-one when he assumed power in 1933. "The party's age make-up," Peukert notes, "provides further confirmation that Nazi members fell 'between' the social classes."[35]

Even as he sought political power Hitler never really thought of himself as the leader of an ordinary political party. During the last election held before he assumed power—an election in which Hitler himself, as the head of a coalition government, precipitated—he never offered political programs that would address the interests of the varied segments of the electorate. In that last election campaign, from which the Nazis gained only a plurality of the Reichstag seats despite a campaign rhetoric of impending civil war that culminated in the burning of the Reichstag and blamed on the Communists, Hitler did not conceal his disdain for political programs. Bullock points out that at Munich he said to the voters:

> "Programmes are of no avail, it is the human purpose which is decisive." The Nazi campaign was directed against the record of the fourteen years of party government in Germany, which had "piled mistake upon mistake, illusion upon illusion." What had the Nazis to put in its place? He was no democratic politician, Hitler virtuously replied, to trick the people into voting for him by a few empty promises. "I ask of you, German people, that after you have given the others fourteen years you should give us four."[36]

Hitler was, in effect, asking the German people to blindly sign over to him the future of Germany as a great nation without knowing how that great nation would satisfy their different interests.

While it is usual to think of Nazi supporters as being enthralled by Hitler's charisma, his disdain for formulating political programs reflected something more profound than simply charismatic hubris. As Levy states:

> Contrary to all expectations, the Hitlerites in power . . . dreamed in their way of making the state wither away. The dream, which preceded Hitler's ascension to power, was carried into and sustained throughout his tenure as Führer of the Third Reich. . . . Alfred Rosenberg . . . in a resounding article published in January 1934, proposed . . . the idea of a "total party"—a party that would rule the state, absorb it, and reduce it to the role of a mere instrument. Then Roland Freisler, a few days later . . . advanced the notion of a *Totalvolk,* a *total volkische Idee,* in other words, a totalitarianism based on the mystique of People, Soil, and Race. . . . Their texts are very learned, mobilizing all the worthy resources of Wagnerism and romantic vitalism. . . . He quoted this strong statement from the Führer: "The point of departure of National Socialist doctrine lies not in the state but in the People."[37]

The Nazi leadership always scorned the idea that they were a radically right, Fascist political party that claimed to derive its power from the people. It did not represent the people; it was a representation of the dream of a people who wanted to become the people that the laws of nature destined them to become. At the beginning of her analysis of totalitarianism in *The Origins of Totalitarianism,* Arendt states:

> Nothing is more characteristic of the totalitarian movements in general and of the quality of fame of their leaders in particular than the startling swiftness with which they are forgotten and the startling ease with which they can be replaced. . . . This impermanence no doubt has something to do with the proverbial fickleness of the masses and the fame that rests on them; more likely it can be traced to the perpetual-motion mania of totalitarian movements which can remain in power only so long as they keep moving and set everything around them in motion.[38]

Arendt is shifting our attention away from the image that captures our fancy (fantasy?) that the leader, standing rock solid on his platform above the enthralled cheering masses, is a fetish for the eternal stolid father whose presence stabilizes the uncertain world of his children. There is no question, as Arendt points out, "that the totalitarian regimes, so long as they are in power, and the totalitarian leaders, so long as they are alive, 'command and rest on mass support' up to the end."[39] What is implied by Arendt, however, is that the enthrallment with the leader that is so essential to totalitarian regimes is not enthrallment with a power to stabilize the meaning of the world, but with a power that sets the signs of everything that once marked a stable, meaningful world into bewildering motion. From the beginning, Arendt points out, the Nazis conceptualized their ascendancy to power as "the work of undermining actively existing institutions" and, in Hitler's own terms, "the decomposition of the status quo."[40] The purpose of this undermining of existing institutions was not to replace them. Stern points out that Hitler's "originality consists in a deliberate reversal of the functions normally attributed [to] personal– existential values on the one hand and social–political values on the other. . . . Politics, in the scheme Hitler evolved, is personalized, whereas all impersonal aspects of politics, including its stable institutions and its foundation in the rule of law, are designated as 'abstract,' 'bureaucratic,' or 'unauthentic.'"[41] Once in power, everything should mean something other than what it once meant, and no meaning of anything should endure. This decomposing of meaning was affected on a number of fronts simultaneously, constituting the thrust of what was called the Nazi Revolution.

The Nazi rise to power is rightly reckoned to be a revolutionary mass movement spearheaded by those who had become alienated and indifferent to political life because of the social chaos brought on by the end of World War I and the Weimar Republic. But, Arendt observes, there are "decisive differences between nineteenth-century mob organizations and twentieth-century mass movements. . . . [N]one of their nineteenth-century predecessors . . . ever involved their members to the point of complete loss of individual claims and ambition, or had ever realized that an organization could succeed in extinguishing individual identity permanently and not just for the moment of collective heroic action."[42]

The Nazi rise to power may have been a revolution, but its purpose was not to reconstitute a social and political system with which their followers could identify and derive a personal identity. Totalitarianism sweeps away the roadmarks that establish continuity with the previous social world and its followers' sense of individual identity. Hitler consistently presented himself in the image of the agent who would clean up the social, economic, and political mess of the past that caused the terrible suffering of the German people. Because he defined himself as the figure who transcended the decadent corruption of everyday life, we readily think of him as distant from the German people, buffered from them by lesser party functionaries. But just the reverse is true. Hitler was the buffer between lesser party functionaries, who suffered from the residual distrust of corrupt politicians that Hitler exploited for his revolution, and the German People. As Kershaw put it: "Hitler was regarded as the personification of the nation and the unity of the 'national community,' aloof from the selfish sectional interests and material concerns which marked the normality of 'everyday life' and created the damaging divisions in society and politics—the selfless exponent of the national interest, whose incorruption and unselfish motives were detachable from the scandalous greed and hypocrisy of the party functionaries."[43] It was the potency of Hitler's detachment, for example, that carried the party through the consternation in the general population caused by the 1934 bloody purges of the Sturmabteilung (SA).

The Nazis replaced the old class structure of the nation with a Volkisch racial structure. But this racial structure did not give a stable meaning to the world. Identity could no longer be reckoned in traditional terms of having a German character superior to non-German peoples by virtue of inheriting the culture and language of the nation in which one was born and lived. It was now a question of defining who one was in terms of having the pure blood of the Aryan-Germanic race coursing through one's veins. The *other,* from whom one differentiated oneself, was no longer the competing French or English claims of superior character but rather the Jew, who in his pernicious cunning had defiled through the centuries the Aryan-Germanic race. But who was an Aryan and who was a Jew? An entire nation became obsessed with increasingly refined physiognomic measurements and with obsessively sifting through family lineages in a way that in retrospect looks like a dark, farcical comedy. But it is never a farce to a nation that structures itself along racial lines, because what is at stake is the attempt to stabilize the meaning of identity that must always remain in motion.

Burleigh and Wipperman recount that:

> In a novel, published in 1918, entitled *Sin Against the Blood,* [Artur Dinter] told the story of a "racially pure" blonde, blue-eyed German woman who was seduced by a Jew. Although she later managed to get away from him, and subsequently married an "Aryan," she and her husband nonetheless produced "typically Jewish-looking" children. Her "hereditary properties" had been permanently corrupted by a casual encounter with a Jew. This salacious and quasipornographic nonsense was sold in hundreds of thousands of copies.[44]

It was only one of many of those kind of novels that were immensely popular after World War I, which no doubt came to haunt the German consciousness when it became a racially structured nation. The perfect race was a concept that could only have meaning in the future tense. The identity of the present Volk fell in that ambiguous space between the past and the future. This was gospel in *Mein Kampf,* where Hitler stated that the perfect race would be realized only after eliminating the "six-hundred-year obstruction of the reproductive capacities and possibilities to reproduce of the physically degenerate and the mentally ill."[45] How could it be otherwise? Despite his blue eyes, neither Hitler himself nor his chief minions, Goebbels, Bormann, Himmler, Goering, or Hess, resembled ideal Aryan-types. They, of course, did not have to; they were the will to realize the future.

The restructuring of the life of the nation along racial lines was not perceived as a political act. The distinction between the political world and the world it governs—the bedrock of the history of the modern nation–state—was kept ambiguous by the Nazis. There was only a porous boundary between where one began and the other ended. As Arendt puts it:

> Himmler who knew so well the mentality of those whom he organized, described not only his own SS-men, but the large strata from which he recruited them, when he said they were not interested in "everyday problems" but only "ideological questions of importance for decades and centuries, so that the man . . . [*sic*] knows he is working for a great task which occurs but once in 2000 years." The gigantic massing of individuals produced a mentality which, like Cecil Rhodes some forty years before, thought in continents and felt in centuries.[46]

The meaning of everything was kept in motion so that it proved nearly impossible to formulate clear judgments about the regime's actions. It was not a matter of lying about things to the people. While Hitler was a pragmatist as well as, some have suggested, a brilliant planner when the occasion demanded, he did not think of himself as the head of a stable, enduring totalitarian regime; his will was the conduit for realizing a vision that would end the very idea of a political regime. The ability to evaluate by political criteria actions that once would have been clearly defined as political was lost for both those who acted and the masses toward whom action was directed. The regime, each of its layered, doubled, and multiplied organs of authority being extensions of the Leader who means not something to everyone but everything to everyone, is unable to evaluate itself.

The hallmark of the regime was its unpredictability, often to the people and many times even to itself. When the Russian campaign began, Padfield notes, "[t]he German people were utterly astonished. Yet it was not for long. If the next SD [Sicherheitsdienst] secret report is to be believed, the initial shock gave way within hours, the very afternoon of that fatal Sunday, 22 June, to the unanimously held conviction that the Reich government could not have acted otherwise. That was what Hitler told them. There was 'especially strong sympathy for the Führer, who had to keep silent so long before his Volk.'"[47] This sympathy towards Hitler had been constant from the beginning. During 1934, Kershaw notes, "[a]mong the peasantry, sections of the lower middle class, and not least among industrial workers and the millions still unemployed, the feeling grew that the economic reality of the Third Reich bore scant relation to its popularity."[48] Nevertheless, 1934 was a triumphant year for the Nazis, culminating in the massive party rally at Nuremberg that was filmed by Riefenstahl.

Arendt points out that the Nazi administrative structure was kept "in a state of fluidity which permits it constantly to insert new layers and define new degrees of militancy. The whole history of the Nazi party can be told in terms of new formations within the Nazi movement."[49] It is as if the hierarchy of administrative and planning organs was constantly being invented and reinvented, thereby keeping the meaning of its bureaus, bodies, and services in perpetual motion.

This was true for the Nazi administration of its core racial policy. Hitler's outline of his racial program led to a proliferation of competing state and party agencies eager to plan its details and implement it. Even Himmler, who eventually gained control over it, could not control it completely. Burleigh and Wipperman note that "ad hoc groups were formed for particular aspects of Nazi racial policy . . . [such as] the systematic mass murder of the mentally and physically handicapped."[50] Even the 16-million-member NSV, the so-called social arm of the party, was involved in the planning and implementation of racial policy. This kind of organizational confusion suggests that behind every concrete governmental agency lurked another metaphysical agency—whatever it was that was moving Germany to fulfill its destiny and fate. Hitler, at least up to a point, seemed relatively indifferent to the confusing invention of agencies, bureaus, advisory groups, and the like, with their attendant power struggles that marked the Nazi administrative structure in general. In his vision it would all wither away in time like the nation–state itself.

It is precisely the link Arendt draws between power and the destabilization of meaning that establishes the puzzle of the Nazi regime. If the meaning of everything is always in perpetual motion, if every plan promulgates unpredictability, what keeps everything from falling apart?

The puzzle is not simply structural, in a strict sociological sense, but rather how to understand the loyalty of individuals to a regime that by destabilizing the meaning of everything that surrounds people destabilizes the meaning of the self to itself. Totalitarianism not only decomposes the political structures associated with the modern nation–state it replaces, but also the terms inherited with modernity by which the self has come to think of itself: as developing into an autonomous reasoning self standing motionless in the midst of an ephemeral world, analyzing and revealing the motionless causes of motion.

When Arendt shows us that Nazism was unprecedented because its actions refused its own past—i.e., it carried its past across a line that divided it from its past—she shows us that it was a movement that did not depend on loyalty to a vision of another world that could be reached by leaving this one behind, but to a vision of this world reached by purifying it of its corrupting terror. The world dominated by a superior race was the sign of a purified world. The actions of the Nazi movement did not justify itself in terms of a law that reached for its followers' loyalty. Its actions *were* the law, speaking the only language the law could speak:

> It is the monstrous, yet seemingly unanswerable claim of totalitarian rule that, far from being "lawless," it goes straight to the sources of authority from which all positive laws—based on "natural law," or on customs and tradition, or on the historical event of divine revelation—receive their ultimate legitimation. . . . Totalitarian lawfulness, executing the laws of Nature or History, does not bother to translate them into standards of right and wrong for individual human beings, but applies them directly to the "species," to mankind. The laws of Nature or History, if properly executed, are expected to produce as their end a single "Mankind," and it is this expectation that lies behind the claim to global rule of all totalitarian governments.[51]

It is the uncanny, blind, unthinking loyalty of the German people to the unprecedented actions of the Nazi regime that were experienced as the performance of an inexorable law that carries us beyond the Final Solution, beyond the horrific actions of savages dressed up as SS and supported by a population gulled by a viciously effective propaganda machine, to the heart of understanding its significance for our time.

Only when we understand the blind loyalty that made the Final Solution possible will we understand its significance, and we will understand this blind loyalty only when we grasp that it was not loyalty to a political program of a political regime.

~ **3** ~

It was a new experience of loyalty that the Nazi movement commanded. Raul Hilberg's insight that the Nazis had to invent their mode of bureaucratic murder as they went along can be applied to everything the Nazis did. They were inventing the belief in the invention of that which had never been experienced before. At the center of every possibility, Arendt tells us, "as the motor that swings it into motion, sits the Leader. He is separated from the elite formation by an inner circle of the initiated who spread around him an aura of impenetrable mystery which corresponds to his 'intangible preponderance.'"[52] Hitler's mysterious "intangible preponderance" was not a function of his distance from the people, but of his intimate closeness to them. He was dispersed among the layered, doubled, and multiplied organs of governmental authority that surrounded them everywhere.

Hitler's charisma did not flow from some distant dark space he occupied on a horizon beyond the world that his followers experienced. The space he occupied was a space he shared with the people to whom he called to move beyond a dissolving world. His charisma did not flow from a point of dark mystery inside him, but from a point of fusion between himself and the German people. Contrary to common belief, totalitarianism for Arendt:

> [E]liminates the distance between the rulers and the ruled and achieves a condition in which power and the will to power, as we understand them, play no role, or at best a secondary role. In substance, the totalitarian leader is nothing more nor less than the functionary of the masses he leads; he is not a power-hungry individual imposing a tyrannical and arbitrary will upon his subjects. . . . Without him they would lack external representation and remain an amorphous horde; without the masses the leader is a nonentity. . . . Hitler was of the opinion that . . . "thinking exists only by virtue of giving or executing orders" and thereby elimi-

nated even theoretically the distinction between thinking and acting on the one hand, and between the rulers and the ruled on the other.[53]

The elimination of the distinction was not just theoretical. Hitler's speeches did not call for the German people to agree with him about anything. They were designed, Stern points out, for an effect:

> Here at last myth and reality are one: seen as a whole, the speech is a per-locutionary act. It claims for the present moment a greater national cohesion (a closer *"Volksgemeinschaft"*) than Germany has known in all the centuries of her history, and through its very act of affirmation the claim is made good. . . . Solidarity and agreement are *expressed and thus achieved* [Stern's emphasis] even before it has become quite clear what precisely the agreement is about. The audience is not being informed, it is made to perform; and its performance "makes history"[54]

We hear an intimation of what was being performed in Leni Riefenstahl's hysterical imagery, transferred eventually to her signature film, *The Triumph of the Will,* in terms of which she recollected, over fifty years later, the first time she heard Hitler give a speech. She said she had experienced "an almost apocalyptic vision. . . . It seemed as if the earth's surface were spreading out in front of me, like a hemisphere that suddenly splits apart in the middle, spewing out an enormous jet of water, so powerful that it touched the sky and shook the earth. I felt quite paralysed."[55]

The expression of "solidarity and agreement" staged by Hitler's speeches was like an act of giving birth; something consequential was being born, not dreamt of being born. What makes Riefenstahl's *The Triumph of the Will* an eerily uncanny film despite its inordinate length is not its military pomp, which by itself has the kind of comically grotesque overtones played on by Chaplin in *The Great Dictator* or Zero Mostel in *The Producers,* but that its drama being watched is like the unfolding of a fusion between Hitler and his audience, including Riefenstahl herself while filming it.

We hear something of this strange fusion between Hitler and the German people echoed in the reflections of a gray-haired Rotarian remembering, fifty years later, the night Hitler won an election victory in 1933 in the little town of Detmold: "You must have seen the sea of flags, the cheering crowds, the tremendous enthusiasm. I'll never forget it myself. I've never seen so many ecstatic faces in my entire life. People were wild with joy. . . . And you know, it was all handled quite correctly and with perfect discipline. . . ."[56] "Disciplined joy," a strangely oxymoronic phrase, holds the promise of elation through the discipline of collective action because it suggests that joy *is* the discipline of a collective act fused to Hitler's will.

Hitler embodied the will that did not have to explain itself. In this sense, at least, he was a creature of modernity. The will, which Arendt calls the "mental organ for the future,"[57] became the paramount characteristic in the modern age of being human "because the modern age's main and entirely new concept, the notion of *Progress* as the ruling force in human history, placed an unprecedented emphasis on the future."[58] The idea of progress, emphasizing "things neither necessary nor sempiternal would expose men of thought to the contingency of all things human more radically and more mercilessly than ever before." The problem "found its pseudo-solution in the nineteenth century *philosophy of history*, whose greatest representative worked out an ingenious theory of a hidden reason and meaning in the course of world event, directing men's wills in all their contingency toward an ultimate goal they never intended."[59]

Hitler never meant his speeches to convey an analytical mind, but rather a powerful will. Hitler embodied movement toward a future that need not be reasoned about because *willing* commanded *reasoning* and *willing* was the representative of the disembodied cosmic process of evolution. The future was not something to be dreamed about because it lay close at hand, within reach, across an infinitesimal gap readily crossed by those with the will to do so. The will that Hitler represented was not the will to power of a demagogic tyrant, but a will that with words innervated the will of the masses with a disciplined joy to enact great, inexorable events. "[S]ounded words," Kristin Neuschel points out, "have power because they cannot be conceived as things that can somehow exist in a neutral space between persons; they are not separated from human animateness. . . . Cultures with a primarily oral experience of language have been described as 'verbomotor' because they attend not simply to words but to words in conjunction with actions."[60]

A speaker rarely experiences himself or is experienced by his listeners as separate from his words as is a writer. A written text can dissipate the will of a writer because it brings the reader into the scene of meaning as an interpreter in a way that a listener is not. "Oral expression is typically made up of formulaic clusters of words rather than of infinitely varying combination of words."[61] Hitler's well-known formulaic redundancy in his speeches, containing what Neuschel has generally termed "retrievable words" without which "sense cannot be made out of a succession of thoughts,"[62] is sometimes described as having given his speeches a monotonous, haranguing quality. This is the quality, to the ears of the people of Western democracies, that seems to provoke a waiting for politicians to prove that they have a will behind their rhetoric. But it is the formulaic redundancy of Hitler's speeches that limited the need to interpret what he said, establishing without equivocation that he meant what he said, and that what he was conveying was *his* will and *his* alone, subordinate to no one and nothing but the destiny of Germany and Das Volk that was speaking through him. Who can doubt the power of that will when Speer tells us that the last concert he, Speer, arranged, which he thought might be the last he would ever hear because it was being played before a packed house as Russian guns were pounding Berlin to rubble, featured the last movement of *Götterdämmerung?*[63]

Loyalty to the Nazi regime meant loyalty to Hitler; and loyalty to Hitler meant loyalty to an incarnation of one's own will. Such a loyalty, Arendt points out, must be a selfless loyalty: "[T]he disturbing factor in the success of totalitarianism is . . . the true selflessness of its adherents. . . . To the wonder of the whole civilized world, he may even be willing to help in his own prosecution and frame his own death sentence if only his status as a member of the movement is not touched. . . . Identification with the movement and total conformism seem to have destroyed the very capacity for experience, even if it be as extreme as torture or the fear of death."[64]

To meet the demand for total loyalty to the regime, individuals must identify with a regime that represents the direction toward which the meaning of everything that is in motion, including the structures of the regime itself, is moving. This is not identification with the substance of the regime, since its substance is constantly composing and decomposing its meaning, but with the decomposing process itself. Arendt sees that what makes an identification with such a process possible is that totalitarianism creates a fictional world filled with overwhelming terrors as the reality of a world that must be destroyed. "Hitler's rule over the Germans" Jäckel stresses, "did not in any way rest solely or even predominantly on the use of terror."[65] The German people as a whole did not experience National Socialism as a source of terror, but as their salvation from terror. As Arendt puts it:

> The trouble with totalitarian regimes is not that they play power politics in an especially ruthless way, but that behind their politics is hidden an entirely new and unprecedented concept of power, just as behind their *Realpolitik* lies an entirely new and unprecedented concept of reality. Supreme disregard for immediate consequences rather than ruthlessness; rootlessness and neglect of national interests rather than nationalism; contempt for utilitarian motives rather than unconsidered pursuit of national interest; idealism, i.e., their unwavering faith in an ideological fictitious world, rather than lust for power. . . .[66]

To be loyal to the totalitarian movement is to be loyal to the idea that those who are loyal are superior realists compared to others everywhere else who cannot struggle to move the world toward a final solution of the terrors that threaten to overwhelm it, but only suffer their terrors mutely. This is what Arendt means when she speaks of Nazi rule by "means of dominating and terrorizing human beings from within."[67] Everything that gives and supports a political regime identity as a regime—a mission that bestows on it its command of power to defend the virtue of its people who are its followers from their enemies—is specious and false. The world has always been divided between those who love power for its own sake and those who give power to them. But everything that flowed from the commonsensible meaning of the political reality of the world has been false. The only real thing about the world has been that it is a world of terror. It is not a world that political processes can change, because political change only repeats the specious structure of the world. Change is the false dream of modernity—the dream of progressive continuity toward the full realization of the individual. That specious world must die in its entirety. The meaning of everything taken as commonsense reality—politics, the individual, those who govern and are governed—will be erased as the specious world dies.

The totalitarian movement, shrouded in the mystery of meaning constantly in motion, formulates an ideological narrative that conveys the source and identity of the vague, inarticulate terrors to which people who live in the everyday world are exposed. Anti-Semitism had a different meaning to the Nazis than it had in its own time because the Jews who had been known as a national problem that had to be solved by political means were now defined as the problem of terror at the center of a fictional world of solutions by terror that mandated their extermination. Identifying the Jews in these terms did not present a problem; their predecessors were already in place. The nineteenth century had already argued, Daniel Pick points out, that "[p]rogress . . . threw up various biological unfortunates in its remorseless wake. The mad, the criminal, the discontented and the perverse were the evolutionary baggage borne by the modern state."[68]

Evolutionary baggage is not the best metaphor. In Pick's own terms, they were not just inferior-types cast off by evolutionary progress, but the dark side of the idea of progress, posing a threat to it:

> The later Victorian period undoubtedly did witness a multifaceted crisis of self-representation: and that crisis was often specifically articulated in terms of "degeneration.". . . [A]long side . . . confident predictions [of progress] lay unresolved and increasingly intense worries about evolutionary regression. . . . Degenerationist argument was not only used to describe other "races" (who in European racial theory had long been supposed to have degenerated from the "ideal physique" of the "white races"), but also to envision internal dislocation and disorder within European societies.[69]

The Nazi rhetoric of degeneration carried beyond social dislocation and disorder. Those, like Jews, who represented degenerative-types were defilers of the social body that was struggling to progress; and with "defilement," Ricouer once had occasion to remark, "we enter into the reign of terror."[70] The Nazi language depicting Jews as disease was not meant to be the hyperbole of invective but a literal identification. The disease was not something that was carried by the Jews—they *were* the disease. The disease was not specific but all the more terrifying because it was indefinite; it was everywhere, concealed in every Jewish act, constantly changing form. In a speech as early as 1919 Hitler referred to Jewish power that "effortlessly and interminably multiplies" as a "racial tuberculosis among nations."[71] But this is an idea, Susan Sontag shrewdly observes, in which "there is already something easily transferred to cancer." Or, as she also observes, to gangrene that has "some of the same metaphoric properties as cancer—it starts from nothing; it spreads; it is disgusting. . . ."[72]

Every physician knows that when he confronts his patient he is confronting the patient's idea of disease as an event taking place within the invisible confines of the body. Because it has no definite shape for the patient, it is a fantastic event without limits that produces the sensation of terror. The physician's power emanates, of course, from his expert ability to make the interior of the body visible, which then allows him to give the disease a name that translates something terrifying into something merely frightening. But the patient knows two things that the physician probably knows as well but can conceal even to himself behind the armor of his professional expertise: First, that every effect of a known disease is the possibility of an effect produced by something as yet unknown that lies in wait in the future; and second, that science itself, whose other name is *progress* towards making the invisible visible, always is open to a future that admits the possibility of the reverse. It is as if the Nazis, identifying at the beginning with the disaffected, alienated, and marginal segments of the German population, knew that it is only with difficulty that terror relents to mere fear, because fear condemns a tear in the fabric of order, while terror condemns order itself as a fragile tissue of lies.

The Jew was the secret, invisible invader whose tiniest foothold in the social body, the beachhead established by the single obscure, invading organism, the splitting of a single obscure, rogue cell, would lead to a terrifying, agonizing death. If this was the problem, then there was no partial solution to the problem of the Jews. It is a mistake to think of the Final Solution as a war against the Jews. It fails on two counts according to Scarry's definition of war: "[F]irst, that the immediate activity is injuring; second, that the immediate activity of war is a contest."[73]

The Final Solution was beyond the inflicting of injury, and it was not a contest. There is no victory involved, no surrender of the injured to the threat of further injury, nor was there the possibility of the Nazis losing the contest. The extermination of the Jews was precisely what the Nazi euphemism claimed it to be: The final solution of a problem defined by living Jews. And the action required to solve that problem is the same as the action needed to solve any problem: work. Arad's metaphor of a Nazi "extermination machine"[74] is apt, not only because of the systematic organization of the Final Solution but because extermination *was* work—a particular kind of work blending with the violence of total war, demanding everybody's involvement because the problem of the Jews is the problem of the assault of terror on life itself. Everyone must work on solving such a problem with a work that cannot end at day's end. This was proclaimed by Hitler himself, as all such matters were proclaimed: "National Socialism is not a doctrine of inertia but a doctrine of conflict. Not a doctrine of happiness and good luck, but a doctrine of work and a doctrine of struggle, and thus also a doctrine of sacrifice."[75]

In every respect the SS, assigned to execute the Final Solution, followed Hitler's doctrine. They expressed this with those notorious signs on the gates to Dachau and Auschwitz: "Arbeit Macht Frei." "[W]ith Himmler," Padfield tells us, "it was not even an irony. The same went for the slogan he had painted later along the pitched roof of the long utility building built by the prisoners facing the huts along the *Appelplatz* [in Dachau]: 'There is one way to freedom. Its milestones are: obedience, zeal, honesty, order, cleanliness, temperance, truth, sense of sacrifice and love of the Fatherland.'"[76] Intending no irony, the message "Arbeit Macht Frei" was intended for the two groups of occupants of the camps: the prisoners and the guards. It told the prisoners that the compulsions they live under are not compulsions imposed by the power of the police, but the necessity of the destiny of the Reich that carries the future of the world, and for which they, the prisoners, are destined to work and die as the only way they can redeem themselves as subhumans. It told the guards that they too are under precisely the same necessity spelled out by the signs to embody the virtues that would redeem the world from its failure to realize its destiny. The murder of the Jews was a necessary medical work to heal the terrifying injuries they did to the body of the people. The hospitals at Auschwitz and Dachau were symbols of that medical work. It was Himmler himself, after all, who patronized, witnessed, and even suggested the grotesque medical experiments performed at Dachau.

The German people epitomized an uncanny loyalty that was blind to the meaning of a work that refused to define murder as its limits. Both individual members of the SS and the nation experienced a terrible solitariness if they dared to stop working in that fictional world, where the horizon is narrowed to the presence of terror everywhere and where the meaning of everything is in motion, to think about the meaning of themselves in relation to the work demanded of them. They thought about their work in the way in which any work demands thought, but their loyalty proscribed thinking about the meaning of themselves working. Their loyalty was not to the political regime that directed the movement, but to a fictional world of terror. The regime never seemed unduly anxious over the paradox of keeping the people's loyalty blind to the unprecedented horrific violence of their extermination machine, whose invention and every phase of operation depended on involving those selfsame people. Loyalty to the fictional world of terror made blindness irrelevant: The totalitarian world of terror, Arendt points out, "simply and mercilessly presses men, such as they are, against each other so that the very space of free action . . . disappears. . . . If the undeniable automatism of historical or natural happenings is understood as the stream of necessity, whose meaning is identical to its law of movement and therefore quite independent of any event . . .," then events themselves, of whatever sort, "can only be considered as a superficial and transitory outburst of the deep permanent law. . . ."[77]

Elias Canetti, while not distinguishing between *fear* and *terror,* nevertheless helps us grasp the relationship between the way terror presses people together to erase the space of free action, their blind loyalty, and the indifference of the Nazi regime to whether the events of the Final Solution were secret or not:

> There is nothing that man fears more than the touch of the unknown . . . . He wants to *see* what is reaching towards him, and to be able to recognize or at least classify it. . . . It is only in a crowd that man can become free of this fear of being touched. That is the only situation in which the fear changes into its opposite. The crowd he needs is the dense crowd, in which body is pressed to body; a crowd too whose psychical constitution is also dense, or compact, so that he no longer notices who it is that presses against him. As soon as a man has surrendered himself to a crowd, he ceases to fear its touch. Ideally, all are equal there; no distinctions count, not even that of sex. The man pressed against him is the same as himself. He feels him as he feels himself. Suddenly it is as though everything were happening in one and the same body. . . . Only together can men free themselves of the burdens of dis-

tance; and this precisely is what happens in a crowd. . . . In that density, where there is scarcely any space between, and body presses against
body, each man is as near to the other as he is to himself; and an
immense feeling of relief ensues. It is for the sake of this blessed
moment, when no one is greater or better than another, that people
become a crowd.[78]

It is, Arendt reminds us, the very *practicality* of a fictional world of
terror that allowed for a blind loyalty to the extermination machine that
could not have been blind: "Practically speaking . . . terror in all cases,
executes on the spot the death sentences which Nature has already pro-
nounced on unfit races and individuals . . . without waiting for the slow-
er and less efficient elimination which would presumably be brought
about anyhow."[79]

$\sim$ **4** $\sim$

While Arendt's insights into the unprecedented nature of totalitarian
regimes has been seen as having some value for measuring how totalitarianism deviates from other political regimes, they have been criticized for not being helpful for explaining the deviation itself. This is
certainly true, but it is true because Arendt never defined totalitarianism as a problem to be explained. *Understanding,* for Arendt, was not
a term equivalent to *explanation,* but contrary to it. Her opposition to
a science of history based on causal explanations is unequivocal. For
example: "Causality . . . is an altogether alien and falsifying category
in the historical sciences" and "[w]hoever in the historical sciences
honestly believes in causality actually denies the subject matter of his
own science."[80] Her explications of what she means, however, are
invariably condensed and confusing, leaving unanswered the question:
*If she does not want to equate understanding with explanation, what
does she want?*

The question is a crucial one to which we shall have to return again
and again because we confront it at virtually every point in her work.
There is an answer that she provides, but never in the form of a systematic methodological or philosophical statement; it is dispersed, rather, in
different contexts. Perhaps Arendt was right to leave her answer context-

dependent, for it gains a certain significance that way. In the present context, however, where understanding the unprecedented nature of totalitarianism is at issue, it is not very illuminating to be told, as Arendt does, that the historian, in the last analysis, is a teller of stories: "It is the task of the historian to detect this unexpected *new* with all its implications in any given period and to bring out the full power of its significance. He must know that, though [the historian's] story has a beginning and an end, it occurs within a larger frame, history itself. And history is a story which has many beginnings but no end."[81]

In the same essay, however, in which she states the above, there is a paragraph that, in a highly condensed form, begins to shed a first light on what she means by an "understanding" that is not the equivalent of a causal explanation. Its opening sentence reverses the epistemological basis for causal explanations: "Understanding precedes and succeeds knowledge."[82] To explain the cause of an event means the reverse: knowledge precedes understanding in the sense that we understand an event when we can account for its appearance in terms of principles that can in turn account for the appearance of the general class of events to which it belongs. Our understanding fulfills what Israel Scheffler has called "the ideal of objectivity," which, at least as far as he is concerned, "characterizes not only the scientist, but also the historian, the philosopher, the mathematician, the man of affairs—insofar as all make cognitive claims in a rational spirit."[83] Knowledge can then be said to succeed understanding in the sense that once we know the principles that account for the appearance of a class of events, we know how to control them.

For Arendt, the claim that objective knowledge precedes and succeeds the understanding of events is blind to what the claimant must understand preceding his claim that makes it possible. In other words, objective knowledge that is claimed to be the foundation for understanding has itself a foundation in the assumptions and presuppositions of the one who makes that claim. Being blind to these assumptions and presuppositions fosters a double illusion: First, that understanding flows, as it were, from knowledge to the event that is understood; and second, that the sign of a true understanding is an ability to predict the appearance of the event. For Arendt, lifting that blindness means seeing that understanding events flows toward events from a self-understanding that precedes the claims of objective knowledge, and that the sign of a true understanding is something other than predicting its appearance: "Preliminary understanding, which is at the basis of all knowledge, and true understanding, which transcends it, have this in common: They make knowledge meaningful."[84] *Meaningful* is the operant word here. Arendt is displacing the significance of understanding the Final Solution from the almost obsessive preoccupation we manifest a half-century later over preventing the same kind of event from happening to something else—to understanding its meaning:

> Historical description and political analysis can never prove that there is such a thing as the *nature* or the *essence* of totalitarian government, simply because there is a nature to monarchical, republican, tyrannical, or despotic government. This specific nature is taken for granted by the preliminary understanding on which the sciences base themselves, and this preliminary understanding permeates as a matter of course, but not with critical insight, their whole terminology and vocabulary. . . . If, on the other hand, the scholar wants to transcend his own knowledge—and there is no other way of making knowledge meaningful other than transcending it—he must become very humble again and listen closely to the popular language . . . in order to reestablish contact between knowledge and understanding.[85]

This "humble listening" to the way people experience the common-sense meaning of things, which Arendt seems to suggest is essential for understanding the meaning of totalitarianism, has become impossible today because use of the term has declined almost to the vanishing point. The idea that unprecedented totalitarian regimes pose a challenge to us to make them meaningful has been lost to the idea that they challenge us to explain them as variations in a class of political regimes. Common-sense experience conveyed by the fabric of language that knits people together has been lost as the starting point for meeting the challenge of making something meaningful. The idea that we understand the meaning of an event is absorbed by having an *objective knowledge* of it, and there is nothing humble about possessing objective knowledge—it creates its own language, divorced from commonsense experience of both the people who are expected to live by its commands and those who presume to possess the power of the language that commands.

By stating that the challenge presented by the Final Solution is to understand its meaning, Arendt is not arguing that reality is made by humans, as if humans were like gods. What she is refusing is a commitment to a world of human affairs accounted for by processes in nature in terms of which all the answers to questions about events must be derived. Arendt, in effect, recognizes what Taylor has called the "metaphysical motivation" behind scientific reductionism: "We must avoid anthropocentric properties . . . and give an account of things in absolute terms. . . . [A]bsolute properties . . . are supposedly free of . . . relativity."[86]

Such avoidance, however, is always attached to a very anthropomorphizing faith that to have abstract knowledge of causal processes that precedes and succeeds understanding is to be carried into the future toward the fullness of our humanity. The problem is that the very foundation of that faith, by reducing human actions to the effects of abstract processes, diminishes humans. As Arendt puts it:

> The comparatively new social sciences, which so quickly became to history what technology had been to physics, may use the experiment in a much cruder and less reliable way than do the natural sciences, but the method is the same: they too prescribe conditions, conditions to human behavior, as modern physics prescribes conditions to natural processes. If their vocabulary is repulsive and their hope to close the alleged gap between our scientific mastery of nature and our deplored impotence to "manage" human affairs through an engineering science of human relations sounds frightening, it is only because they have decided to treat man as an entirely natural being whose life process can be handled the same way as all other processes.[87]

The term *totalitarianism* disappeared from use because the question of what it means was answered before it could be asked. The term has no meaning beyond what can be revealed by the comparative study of the processes that cause the appearance, persistence, and disappearance of political regimes. "The process," Arendt states, "which alone makes meaningful whatever it happens to carry along, has thus acquired a monopoly of universality and significance."[88]

Until that monopoly is broken we will not be able to understand the significance of the Final Solution. We can learn nothing about how we experience the problems of our time from explaining the Final Solution as an effect of abstract processes. Arendt provides us with the critical example when, at the beginning of *The Origins of Totalitarianism,* she repeats "a joke that was told after the First World War" which conveys the question, "Why the Jews?" "An antisemite claimed that the Jews had caused the war; the reply was: Yes, the Jews and the bicyclists. Why the bicyclists? asks the one. Why the Jews? asks the other."[89] The question "Why the Jews?" serves as the pretext for Arendt's critique of one of the answers that offers a process explanation: the Nazi project to exterminate the Jews was the culmination of the long history of European anti-Semitism in which Jews served as the scapegoats for tensions and conflicts within and between European polities. It is an appealing answer because the term *scapegoating,* which has an ancient provenance, has been given a scientific imprimatur by the modern social sciences as a pivotal concept (to quote Allport) in "a specific theory of prejudice, namely the frustration theory. . . ."[90]

To describe somebody's prejudice, of course, requires describing his experience. The durability of the scapegoating theory in the social sciences, which gives it the character of a virtual classic, depends on reducing this experience to the action of a process. Allport formulates this action in terms of "three stages: (1) frustration generates aggression; (2) aggression becomes displaced upon relatively defenseless 'goats'; (3) this displaced hostility is rationalized and justified by blaming, projecting, stereotyping."[91] These stages establish the continuity of the Final Solution with the history of European attitudes toward Jews as the secondary effects of the operation of the psychological mechanism, *frustration–aggression.* The group that feels the effect of this process, in Allport's terms, is a "stimulus object presenting traits and practices that are irritating to others."[92] Clearly, Jews fit the bill throughout the history of Europe, but then again, from the vantage point of those who had the power to declare others pariah scapegoats, so did numerous others both within and without the history of the shifting borders of European polities, including Nazi Germany. Scapegoat theory answers the question "Why the Jews?" with a causal formula so general as to suggest that any group would have done for the Nazis, just as, in fact, groups other than Jews did make do as scapegoats in the history of Europe.

Arendt makes it clear that scapegoat theory is not an answer to the "Why the Jews?" question, not because the theory does not apply to the Final Solution—Arendt is not interested in raising the question of the empirical validity of such an explanation—but because applying it yields inane results: "The theory that the Jews are always the scapegoat implies that the scapegoat might have been anyone else as well. It upholds the perfect innocence of the victim, an innocence which insinuates not only that no evil was done but that nothing at all was done which might possibly have a connection with the issue at stake."[93]

The question "Why the Jews?" demands an answer in terms of *reasons* and not *causes*. *Reasons* are not *causes*; *reasons* call for understanding the intentions that actors have in acting toward others, whose specific meaning is inherent in the definition of the goals the actors are purposively pursuing through their actions. *Reasons* call for honoring the complexities that we always perceive surround an historical event, while *causes* call for reducing those complexities to the effects of ahistorical causal mechanisms such as frustration–aggression that are posited to make up part of the universal structure of human psychology. Reducing the history of the Jews in Europe to the history of stimulus objects that renders their history empty of significant content by ignoring no less than the entire field in which history itself unfolds as the complex play of meanings, reasons, and actions between and, one might say, within the plurality of human beings who populate the world.

We are linked to the significance of the Final Solution not because totalitarianism is a potential effect of processes at the political heart of every nation or because genocidal acts are a potential effect of processes that lurk in every human heart. Nothing can deny the possibility that the horrors of the Final Solution can be repeated at any time. But everything in Arendt's work calls attention to this as a source of obfuscation of what is really at stake that links us to the significance of the Final Solution. Its meaning cannot be contained within a framework that explains it as the political act of a regime. No political act, to use Arendt's terms, was ever "based in the last analysis on the conviction that everything is possible—and not just permitted, morally or otherwise, as was the case with early nihilism."[94]

The problem that the Final Solution poses is that it was the unthinking loyalty of virtually an entire nation to this conviction that made it possible. In other words, what links us to the Final Solution is that most-common human experience of loyalty that opens a question suppressed by the ambition to state the causes of the Final Solution: If the experiences of a whole nation's loyalty distorted what was real about their relationship to the world, as if it were a delirium that led them to the Final Solution, how can we know what is real about our own experiences of ourselves and the others who populate the world?

The Final Solution is an inescapable crisis pinned to our time because it moves the debate over doubting our experience of what is real about the meaning of ourselves and others that defines the crisis of our time—moves it from the rarified atmosphere of academia into the everyday world. Every college student today knows that he or she is living in a time that is embroiled in doubting what is real because the meaning of everything is in motion, with the possibility of settling nowhere. But this doubt about what is real becomes everyone's doubt because no one can escape inheriting from the Final Solution the uneasy feeling that to be loyal to some experience of the *real* is to live perhaps in a world where, because everyone is mad, nobody is.

From Arendt's work we learn that we cannot define the Nazis' fictional world of terror in terms of the new ideological beliefs that they created. We cannot say, therefore, that Arendt shows us that the delirium of the German people can be defined in terms of the content of some bizarre belief system. She denies us, in effect, the consoling idea that we can solve the problem of identifying what is a delirious experience solely by what we believe. The solution must lie elsewhere. For Arendt it lies in understanding that the German people's experience of the delirium of loyalty that made possible the Final Solution was a substitute for thinking. In other words, if their delirium of loyalty was a flight from the real to the imaginary, then the failure to think defines the possibility of that flight.

It is with this firmly in mind, we suspect, that Arendt went to Jerusalem to report on Eichmann's trial. By seeing the man sitting in that famous glass box as the failure to think, Arendt had found the terms in which to make the Final Solution significant for us. The terrible question that Eichmann poses for everyone, Jew and non-Jew alike—Will that line that the German people crossed ever be crossed again?—is a question we can never answer. But we can say that an evil like the Final Solution signifies how easy it is for human beings to fail to use their commonplace ability to think. *The banality of evil* makes its appearance in many forms, but always fueled by a delirium of blind loyalty that substitutes for thinking. In this sense, and in this sense only, Arendt saw

Eichmann as Everyman pointing to the need to understand what we mean when we say, in our commonsense language, that we are capable of thinking.

Notes

1. Joyce Appelby, Lynn Hunt, and Margaret Jacob, *Telling the Truth About History* (New York: W.W. Norton, 1994), 10.

2. Berel Lang, *Act and Idea in the Nazi Genocide* (Chicago: University of Chicago Press, 1990), xxi.

3. Quoted in Alvin H. Rosenfeld and Irving Greenberg, eds., *Confronting the Holocaust: The Impact of Elie Wiesel* (Bloomington: Indiana University Press, 1978), 35.

4. Lang, *Act and Idea,* xxi.

5. See Yitzhak Arad, *Belzec, Sobibor, Treblinka: The Operation Reinhard Death Camps* (Bloomington: Indiana University Press, 1987), Part One.

6. Hannah Arendt, *The Life of the Mind* (New York: Harcourt, Brace, Jovanovitch, 1978).

7. For reviews cf. *American Historical Review* 57, no. 4 (1952): 933; *Annals of the American Academy* 277 (1951): 272; *World Politics* 4 (1951–52): 402; and *World Politics* 21 (1968–69): 272.

8. Hannah Arendt, *Essays in Understanding: 1930–1954,* ed. Jerome Kohn (New York: Harcourt Brace, 1993), 402.

9. Arendt, *Essays in Understanding,* 405.

10. Arendt, *Essays in Understanding,* 405.

11. Discussion in *Totalitarianism,* ed. Carl J. Friedrich, Universal Library Ed. (New York: Grosset and Dunlop, 1964), 78.

12. Hannah Arendt, *The Origins of Totalitarianism,* 3d ed. (New York: Harvest/HBJ, 1968), xv.

13. Hannah Arendt, *Eichmann in Jerusalem: A Report on the Banality of Evil,* rev. ed. (New York: Penguin Books, 1977), 4–5.

14. Arendt, *Eichmann in Jerusalem,* 10.

15. Quoted in Clive S. Kessler, "The Politics of Jewish Identity: Arendt and Zionism," in *Hannah Arendt: Thinking, Judging, Freedom,* ed. Gisela T. Kaplan and Clive S. Kessler (Sydney: Allen and Unwin, 1989), 103.

16. Kessler, "The Politics of Jewish Identity," 103.

17. Kessler, "The Politics of Jewish Identity," 103.

18. Arendt, *Eichmann in Jerusalem,* 9–10.

19. Arendt, *The Origins of Totalitarianism,* xi.

20. Arendt, *Essays in Understanding,* 345.

21. Detlev J. K. Peukert, *The Weimar Republic,* tr. Richard Dawson (New York: Hill and Wang, 1992), 160.

22. Marion A. Kaplan, *The Making of the Jewish Middle Class* (New York: Oxford University Press, 1991), 7.

23. Gordon A. Craig, *The Germans* (New York: Meridian Books, 1991), 141.

24. Peukert, *The Weimar Republic,* 158.

25. Peukert, *The Weimar Republic,* 160–61.

26. Eric Hobsbawm, *The Age of Extremes: A History of the World 1914–1991* (New York: Pantheon Books, 1994), 120.

27. Arendt, *Essays in Understanding,* 328.

28. Arendt, *Essays in Understanding,* 345.

29. Arendt, *Essays in Understanding,* 328.

30. Arendt, *Essays in Understanding,* 353.

31. Michael Burleigh and Wolfgang Wipperman, *The Racial State: Germany 1933–1945* (Cambridge, UK: Cambridge University Press, 1991), 25.

32. Arendt, *Essays in Understanding,* 371.

33. Paul Ricouer, *The Symbolism of Evil,* tr. Emerson Buchanan (Boston: Beacon Press, 1967), 5.

34. Peukert, *The Weimar Republic,* 236–37.

35. Peukert, *The Weimar Republic,* 239.

36. Alan Bullock, *Hitler: A Study in Tyranny,* abridged ed. (New York: Harper and Row, 1980), 142–43.

37. Bernard Henri Levy, *The Testament of God,* tr. George Holoch (New York: Harper and Row, 1980), 12.

38. Arendt, *The Origins of Totalitarianism,* 305–6.

39. Arendt, *The Origins of Totalitarianism,* 306.

40. Arendt, *The Origins of Totalitarianism,* 371.

41. J. P. Stern, *Hitler: The Führer and the People* (Berkeley: University of California Press, 1975), 23–24.

42. Arendt, *The Origins of Totalitarianism,* 313–14.

43. Ian Kershaw, *The "Hitler Myth": Image and Reality in the Third Reich* (New York: Oxford University Press, 1987), 253.

44. Burleigh and Wipperman, *The Racial State,* 37.

45. Quoted in Burleigh and Wipperman, *The Racial State,* 40.

46. Arendt, *The Origins of Totalitarianism,* 316.

47. Peter Padfield, *Himmler: Reichsfuehrer—SS* (New York: Henry Holt, 1990), 338.

48. Kershaw, *The "Hitler Myth,"* 64.

49. Arendt, *The Origins of Totalitarianism,* 368.

50. Burleigh and Wipperman, *The Racial State,* 59.

51. Arendt, *Essays in Understanding,* 340.

52. Arendt, *The Origins of Totalitarianism,* 373.

53. Arendt, *The Origins of Totalitarianism,* 325–26.

54. Stern, *Hitler,* 36–37.

55. Quoted in Stefan Kanfer, "Leni Riefenstahl Sees No Evil" in *Civilization* 1, no. 1 (Nov.–Dec. 1994): 47.

56. Berndt Engelmann, *In Hitler's Germany,* tr. Krishna Winston (New York: Pantheon Books, 1986), 9.

57. Arendt, *The Life of the Mind,* vol. 2, 13.

58. Arendt, *The Life of the Mind,* vol. 2, 19.

59. Arendt, *The Life of the Mind,* vol. 2, 28.

60. Kristin Neuschel, *Word of Honor* (Ithaca, NY: Cornell University Press, 1989), 116.

61. Neuschel, *Word of Honor,* 104.

62. Neuschel, *Word of Honor,* 104.

63. Videotape interview with Speer, Episode 21, *The World at War.*

64. Arendt, *The Origins of Totalitarianism,* 307–8.

65. Eberhard Jäckel, *Hitler in History* (Hanover, NH: University Press of New England, 1984), 95–96.

66. Arendt, *The Origins of Totalitarianism,* 417–18.

67. Arendt, *The Origins of Totalitarianism,* 325.

68. Daniel Pick, "The Degenerating Genius," *History Today* 42 (April 1992): 19.

69. Pick, "The Degenerating Genius," 18–19.

70. Ricouer, *The Symbolism of Evil,* 25.

71. Quoted in Susan Sontag, *Illness as Metaphor* (New York: Farrar, Straus, and Giroux, 1978), 83.

72. Sontag, *Illness as Metaphor,* 83, 85.

73. Elaine Scarry, *The Body in Pain* (New York: Oxford University Press, 1985), 63.

74. Arad, *Belzec, Sobibor, Treblinka,* 3.

75. Quoted in Stern, *Hitler,* 33.

76. Padfield, *Himmler,* 134.

77. Arendt, *Essays in Understanding,* 343.

78. Elias Canetti, *Crowds and Power,* tr. Carol Stewart (New York: Seabury Press, 1978), 15–18.

79. Arendt, *Essays in Understanding,* 343.

80. Both quotes can be found in Arendt, *Essays in Understanding,* 319.

81. Arendt, *Essays in Understanding,* 320.

82. Arendt, *Essays in Understanding,* 311.

83. Israel Scheffler, *Science and Subjectivity* (New York: Bobbs-Merill, 1967), 2.

84. Arendt, *Essays in Understanding,* 311.

85. Arendt, *Essays in Understanding,* 311.

86. Charles Taylor, *Human Agency and Language,* vol. 1 of *Philosophical Papers* (Cambridge, UK: Cambridge University Press, 1985), 2–3.

87. Hannah Arendt, *Between Past and Future,* expanded ed. (New York: Penguin Books, 1977), 59.

88. Arendt, *Between Past and Future,* 63–64.

89. Arendt, *The Origins of Totalitarianism,* 5.

90. Gordon Allport, *The Nature of Prejudice,* 25th anniversary ed. (Reading, MA: Addison-Wesley, 1987), 244.

91. Allport, *The Nature of Prejudice,* 350.

92. Allport, *The Nature of Prejudice,* 244.

93. Arendt, *The Origins of Totalitarianism,* 5.

94. Arendt, *Between Past and Future,* 87.

2

The Problem of Thinking

~ 1 ~

After William Shawn, editor of the *New Yorker,* accepted Arendt's pro-
posal that she cover the Eichmann trial, she wrote to the Rockefeller
Foundation to explain why she wanted to change the terms for a grant
she had been awarded: "You will understand why I should cover this
trial; I missed the Nuremberg Trials, I never saw these people in the
flesh, and this is probably my only chance."[1] While it was undoubtedly important for Arendt to see Eichmann, it ultimately proved more
meaningful for her to listen to him. As the former head of Department
IV-D-4 of the SD responsible for Jewish Affairs and Deportations,
Eichmann was charged with fifteen counts of crimes against the Jewish
people, against humanity, and of war crimes. Eichmann pleaded, as
Arendt reports it, "[n]ot guilty in the sense of the indictment." Arendt
then asks a surprising question: "In what sense then did he think he was
guilty?," followed by an equally surprising observation that it is an
"obvious question," which she was the only one to ask: "In the long
cross-examination of the accused, according to him 'the longest ever
known,' neither the defense nor the prosecution nor finally, any of the
three judges ever bothered to ask this obvious question."[2]

The question is not at all obvious. Why should Arendt have heard
Eichmann's plea as the possibility that he might be feeling guilt for acts
committed in the past over which he had never shown signs of hesita-
tion, no less signs of remorse? After all, with unwavering ardor Eichmann had carried out his functions of transporting Jews from every part
of Europe to the killing centers in Poland under difficult wartime conditions. He had returned to an increasingly encircled Berlin from his

39

last assignment in Hungary as late as December 1944, triumphantly declaring Hungary to be "Judenrein" due to the death of over a half-million Jews for which he was directly responsible, even after Auschwitz closed in the Fall of 1944 and rail lines were cut as the Russians advanced on Budapest. Arendt *could* have heard Eichmann's plea, as no doubt the defense, the prosecutor, and the judges did, as not worthy of a query. It was, on the face of it, typical of the plea used in the infamous Nuremberg defense based on the reasons the accused presented for committing acts he did not contest.

Eichmann actually did not disappoint those who had anticipated this defense, including Arendt. Confronted in his pretrial examination, to which Arendt had access, and in his cross-examination, at which she was present, with an incriminating trail of documents and testimony, Eichmann never stopped asserting that he was innocent of committing any crime. He had only obeyed, as any law-abiding citizen must, lawful orders. This could not have been a surprise to Arendt, and had she heard Eichmann's plea as anticipating a Nuremberg defense she would have had no need to question its meaning. That she did question it makes sense only because she had no interest in his defense at all, never doubting for a moment either his guilt or that he deserved to die. Her questioning the meaning of Eichmann's plea signified her interest in understanding Eichmann as a person. In other words, for Arendt, Eichmann's past acts had convicted and sentenced him before the trial began, but what the trial opened to question was the person who had committed those acts. Arendt heard Eichmann's plea not simply as the unoriginal plea that Nazis had made since Nuremberg, but as opening the question of who he *thought* he was in that Jerusalem courtroom—a question that opened the way towards understanding who he was when he had committed his murderous acts over a decade earlier. For the defense, the prosecutor, and the judges the "not guilty" plea alone sufficed to exhaust their interest in Eichmann, because there was no reason for them to be interested in who Eichmann *was* rather than in *what* he had done. If Arendt had come to Jerusalem to "see" the man who bore a great responsibility for the heinous crimes of the Final Solution, his plea certainly prompted her to focus on trying to understand who it was she was looking at by listening to him.

Arendt's ability to listen to Eichmann meant discounting him as the icon of deranged Nazi Jew-haters and -killers as Gideon Hausner, the prosecutor, had once described him: "[A] man obsessed with a dangerous and insatiable urge to kill" and "a perverted, sadistic personality."[3] But Arendt, citing the Israeli psychiatric findings that Eichmann was "normal," curtly dismisses his image as a deranged Jew-killer: "Behind the comedy of the soul experts lay the hard fact that this was obviously no case of moral let alone legal insanity. . . . Worse, his was obviously no case of insane hatred of Jews, of fanatical anti-Semitism or indoctrination of any kind."[4]

More importantly, Arendt's ability to listen to Eichmann meant discounting him as the icon of the modern world—the fabled bureaucratic personality who functions under the bureaucratic principle as Max Weber had formulated it: *sine ira ac studio*. The "specific nature" of bureaucracy, Weber said, "which is welcomed by capitalism, develops the more perfectly the bureaucracy is 'dehumanized,' the more completely it succeeds in eliminating from official business love, hatred, and all purely personal, irrational and emotional elements which escape calculation. This is the specific nature of bureaucracy and it is appraised as its special virtue."[5] It is only a short step, which many have taken, to argue that this virtue is not only the way bureaucrats come to know the job they do, but who they are as virtuous individuals. And only a short step further to arguing that under the Nazi regime this virtue became the instrument for organizing mass murder.

Arendt, while hardly denying Eichmann's obvious administrative skills in the service of mass murder, never takes the step from Weber to Eichmann as a "bureaucratic personality." It is unquestionably true that the Final Solution was made possible by administrative rationality. But the step from the administrative rationality characteristic of the economic enterprises of capitalism to the cause of the Final Solution is too great a step. There is no doubt that there is some truth to the caricature of a bureaucracy manned by those who deliver themselves totally by a selfless loyalty to the rules of an impersonal corporation, but such a picture ignores what it means to speak of a bureaucracy as the administrative arm of government. In an implicit reference to Kafka's work, which Arendt greatly admired, she states that it is

[P]seudomysticism that is the stamp of bureaucracy when it becomes a form of government. Since the people it dominates never really know why something is happening, and a rational interpretation of laws does not exist, there remains only one thing that counts, the brutal naked event itself. What happens to one then becomes subject to an interpretation whose possibilities are endless, unlimited by reason and unhampered by knowledge.[6]

Totalitarian bureaucracy goes beyond pseudomysticism because the bureaucracy of totalitarianism is less the expression of rationality that has gone beyond its limits than of a theory of governance that knows no limits, inventing itself as it moves along, destabilizing the meaning of everything. There are important implications in this for understanding the experience of the bureaucrat. Pawlikowski has observed that: "[t]he fundamental reality that has emerged from my research into the Holocaust is the new sense of human freedom present among the Nazi theoreticians."[7] This "new sense of human freedom" Pawlikowski speaks about among Nazi theoreticians can be translated into a rush of freedom among administrative bureaucrats to be part of a collective action that can realize "the possibility . . . to reshape human society, perhaps humanity itself, to an extent never previously imaginable. The new possibility created a new responsibility—to liberate mankind from the polluters of authentic humanity. . . ."[8]

It was in terms such as these that Arendt heard Eichmann say that he was more than a diminished slave loyal to the rules he was commanded to live by, but an idealist whose loyalty was to the force that moves the history of the world. As Arendt heard it, "he was perfectly sure that he was not what he called an *inere Schweinhund,* a dirty bastard in the depths of his heart; and as for his conscience, he remembered perfectly well that he would have had a bad conscience only if he had not done what he had been ordered to do—to ship millions of men, women, and children to their death with great zeal and most meticulous care. This, admittedly, was hard to take."[9]

But as hard as it was to take Eichmann's claim that his actions attested to his good conscience, she knew it had to be taken seriously. At one point, in what seemed to be only a momentary by-play in the trial, Judge Raveh's eye had been caught by a statement in the transcript of Eichmann's pretrial interrogation. Eichmann, in Arendt's terms, had

[D]eclared with great emphasis that he had lived his whole life according to Kant's moral precepts, and especially according to a Kantian definition of duty. This was outrageous on the face of it, and also incomprehensible, since Kant's moral philosophy is so closely bound up with man's faculty of judgement, which rules out blind obedience. The examining officer did not press the point, but Judge Raveh, either out of curiosity or out of indignation at Eichmann's having dared to invoke Kant's name in connection with his crimes, decided to question the accused. And to the surprise of everybody, Eichmann came up with an approximately correct definition of the categorical imperative. . . . He then proceeded to explain that from the moment he was charged with carrying out the Final Solution he had ceased to live according to Kantian principles, that he had known it, and that he had consoled himself with the thought that he no longer "was master of his own deeds," that he was unable to change anything.[10]

Eichmann, of course, was able to afford himself the consolation of a good conscience despite not living up to Kant's categorical imperative because he had never understood that it stated that the self categorically has the duty to judge its own actions in the light of the transcendental law of reason whose inner voice is the only ground on which the self can claim mastery over its own deeds. Instead, Eichmann had egregiously distorted the categorical imperative to allow for a good conscience while being loyal to another's command of his actions. As Arendt puts it, he had followed the imperative of acting "as if the principle of your actions were the same as that of the legislator or of the law of the land—or, in Hans Frank's formulation . . . 'Act in such a way that the Führer, if he knew your action, would approve it.'"[11]

With a good conscience, Eichmann had found in the Nazi party the definition of the duty he must selflessly perform that fulfilled his self-declared, lifelong ideal to live a moral life. He experienced the absence of mastery over his own deeds as a sacrifice to loyalty and duty. The very experience of making a self-sacrifice identified him to himself as an "idealist," not a "dirty bastard." Furthermore, what identified him as an idealist was that he did not sacrifice himself solely to the desires of his leader. "In Jerusalem," Arendt notes, "Eichmann declared himself to be a *Gottgläubiger,* the Nazi term for those who had broken with Christianity and he refused to take his oath on the Bible. . . ." *Gottgläubigers* like Eichmann "ascribed to a 'higher Bearer of Meaning,' an entity somehow identical with the 'movement of the universe,' to which human life, in itself devoid of 'higher meaning,' is subject."[12] There is an episode of which Arendt was unaware, near the end of Eichmann's life two weeks before his execution, that confirms her observations. Eichmann revealed in a letter to William Hull, an American Evangelist he had agreed to see in prison as his "spiritual advisor," his certain conviction that he was a bearer of this higher meaning: "In my conception, God, *because of his almightiness* [his emphasis], is not a punisher, not an angry God, but rather an all embracing God in whose order I have been placed. And his order [fate] regulates everything. All being and becoming—including me—is *subject* [his emphasis] to this order."[13]

Being a loyal subject was more than a matter of simply believing; it was a matter of willfully living the belief. Arendt reports that

> An "idealist" according to Eichmann's thinking was not merely a man who believed in an "idea" or someone who did not steal or accept bribes, though these qualifications were indispensable. An "idealist" was a man who *lived* for his idea—hence he could not be a businessman—and who was prepared to sacrifice for his idea everything and, especially, everybody. The perfect "idealist," like everybody else, had of course, his personal feelings and emotions, but he would never permit them to interfere with his actions if they came into conflict with his "idea."[14]

And naturally, although he knew he was sending Jews to their death, as an "idealist" Eichmann had no personal proclivity to kill Jews; as an "idealist," he had no recourse but to be loyal to his beliefs by doing his duty.

There was nothing original in anything Arendt heard Eichmann say: neither that unlike some dirty bastards he never had a passion to kill Jews, nor that he knew he was an idealist because he had sacrificed command of his deeds, which did kill Jews, to Hitler, whose commands represented the order of destiny to which everyone was subject. If Eichmann was an icon of anything, he was an icon of the SS, the Schutzstaffel or security units, the most uncanny element in the Nazi regime that seems to endlessly capture our fascination. Eichmann's plea that he should be seen as an idealist and a man of honor was an echo, unfaded by time, of how his chief, Himmler, had seen himself: "Whether our actions run counter to an article (of the law) is of absolutely no consequence to me . . .," he said in 1936. "In fulfilling my task I do basically what I can answer for to my conscience in my work for the Führer and Volk and what conforms to a healthy person's understanding. . . ."[15]

The SS is the kind of service that totalitarian movements must display as the power and worthiness of the leadership to struggle and suffer the doing of what must be done. "Without the elite and its artificially induced inability to understand facts as facts, to distinguish between truth and falsehood, the movement could never move in the direction of realizing its fiction."[16] The elite are super realists who transcend the facts about what causes the world's terror, because while knowledge of that terror must be given to everyone, it takes special qualities to envision, struggle, and suffer what must be done.

Arendt's description of the SS stresses its functions within the movement. As the elite paramilitary force in the Nazi party it was the most militant of the branches of the movement, establishing

> [T]he most efficient of the many protective walls which surround [the movement's] fictitious world, whose "reality" is proved when a member fears leaving the movement more than he fears the consequences of his complicity in illegal actions, and feels more secure as a member than an opponent. This feeling of security, resulting from the organized violence with which the elite formations protect the party members from the outside world, is as important to the integrity of the fictitious world of the organization as the fear of its terror.[17]

This, however, is a thin interpretation of its functions. Heinrich Himmler and his SS minions were also public figures who were meaningful to the people whom they served, displaying the beliefs and values at the heart of the Nazi movement. Originally established in the early 1920's as Hitler's personal bodyguard under Himmler, the SS came to assume control over the security apparatus of the nation, including administration of the concentration camps and later the death camps, as it took responsibility for planning, administering, and implementing the Final Solution. The SS was intended to displace the traditional elite from political power and influence; as Burleigh and Wipperman put it: "Representatives of the traditional elites accepted loss . . . of political power because . . . large factories and landed estates were neither nationalised nor expropriated. New state enterprises were complementary to, rather than in competition with, existing concerns, a form of hybrid supplement to the existing capitalist economy. . . ."[18]

Gaining visibility and prominence by 1931 as a large national organization of over ten thousand members and led by Himmler, whom Hitler regarded as his "Ignatius Loyola," it became clear that the SS was more than a security force. It was the vanguard for reorganizing the nation along racial lines. "Himmler regarded the SS as a male, martial 'order,'" Burleigh and Wipperman tell us:

> [A] bizarre and ahistorical conflation of the Teutonic knights, the Jesuits and Japanese Samurai. They were to be the elite of the National Socialist Party. [Himmler] was personally responsible for the SS's abstruse marriage and birth rituals. These developed into an ersatz religion, complete with pagan kitsch symbolism. . . . Although these rituals seem ridiculous, they deserve to be considered seriously. They contributed to the individuals' self-estimation as part of a carefully selected racial elite superior to all existing aristocracies. . . . The SS was a microcosm of the modern, racially organised, hierarchical, performance-orientated order with which the Nazis wished to replace existing society. The SS would have absorbed or destroyed all alternative bastions of power occupied by the traditional elites.[19]

Himmler recruited SS members indiscriminately from all social classes. Ziegler points out that while "lower middle class recruits accounted numerically for the largest contingent of SS leaders, their proportion matched precisely that found in the general population. Furthermore, almost one-third of Himmler's new knights came from the upper ranks of society, yet this proportion was very low compared to that found in traditional German elites. And finally, though underrepresented vis-à-vis the general population, working class representation was surprisingly high."[20] What was critical, of course, was that SS recruits conform to Aryan racial characteristics, because, as Himmler himself put it, "the SS already marches down the corridor of the heavenly kingdom, or rather the SS is that corridor, for the realization of this kingdom is completely dependent on SS activity."[21]

The SS uniform and the ceremonial displays of its units at national party rallies such as at Nuremberg in 1934 gave the SS a highly visible public profile. While its banners and uniform accessories, such as runes, swords, daggers, etc., called for association with ancient and medieval tradition that made the SS subject to ambivalent, comic feelings, these were erased by the black color of the uniform and the death's head emblem. Taken together with the Nazi armband, the uniform expressed to the German people the unfolding of the somber, terrible mystery of the relationship between death and the destiny of Das Volk. While it was true that SS policy was to keep the Final Solution secret, what they did not want to keep secret was that they were agents of death through which the terrors of the world would be vanquished in order for there to be a future for the world.

Did they actually believe that their policy of secrecy would be effective? Given that it took the resources of the entire nation to design, construct, and operate their extermination machine, it would have been a bizarre hallucination if they did. The function of secrecy was to weld the members of the SS to a metaphysical if not mystical dimension that it was essential for them to publicly display but, like magicians performing on stage, never explain. This is reflected in Himmler's infamous Posen speech to the SS generals on October 4, 1943. Alluding to what was involved in implementing the Final Solution, he reassures the generals: "Most of you know what it means to look at 100 corpses, 500 corpses, 1,000 corpses. Having borne that and nevertheless—some exceptional human weaknesses aside—having remained decent [*anstandig geblieben zu sein*] has hardened us." By having "remained decent" Himmler means that they had not been infected by the Jews:

> The wealth they [the Jews] had, we have taken. I gave strict orders—which SS Gruppenfuhrer Pohl has carried out—that this wealth be promptly transferred to the Reich. We have taken nothing. . . . [W]e do not have the right to enrich ourselves, no matter if it were only a fur, a watch, a mark, a cigarette, no matter what it might be. While eliminating a germ, when all is said and done, we do not wish to become infected by the germ and to die from it. I will not allow the least zone of infestation to form or to become established. Wherever it is formed, we shall burn it out together [*werden wir sie gemeinsam ausbrennan*].[22]

Telling his SS that they had become "hardened" by their work of murder was congratulating them on having passed a critical test of character. There had been SS who refused to join in the killing. But there is no official record that they were ever punished or suffered official recrimination.[23] What was in question was their ability to suffer a work that required "nerves of steel."[24] Their failure was a lack of hardness to suffer that work, and this lack, rather than the softness of too much moral doubt, defined the cardinal sin of being unable to act. In addition, as in the case of someone who lapses from attending religious services, the door was left open for redemption, because the lapse does not by itself indicate a betrayal of the belief. They would always remain part of what Himmler once described as "a Knightly Order, from which one cannot withdraw, to which one is recruited by blood and within which one remains with body and soul so long as one lives on this earth."[25] How could it be otherwise? To have been admitted to membership in the SS in the first place was the sign that one had an invisible quality of character that no visible lack of steel nerves could erode.

This invisible quality of character is what Himmler tells his generals they have demonstrated when he tells them that the murder they accomplished "is a glorious, unwritten page of our history, one that will never be written. . . . Altogether, however, we can say that we have accomplished the most difficult task for the love of our people. And we have not sustained any damage to our inner self, our soul and our character [*und wir haben keinen Schaden in userem Inneren, in unserem Seele, in unserem Charakter daran genommen*]."[26] By assigning their murderous deeds to an "unwritten page in history," Himmler probably does not mean that the Final Solution will be a hidden secret because all signs of and witnesses to it will be obliterated. He probably means rather that you cannot write a history about what is accomplished by the inner self, the soul, and the purity of character that is part of the eternal that has no history and already contains within it the future as destiny. History can be written only about what is visible, which of course is the history of the Nazi movement that embodies the will to reach toward that destined future. In that history the SS will occupy its page as Himmler's Knights whose mission is to struggle for existence—a struggle that is in defense of those eternal verities that make existence meaningful and worthwhile that are threatened by the disease of the Jews.

It is this terrifying threat that absorbs the loyalty of the SS and the German people to the leader of a movement whose only law is a mindless loyalty to a work that knows no limits. It was a blind loyalty that Hitler and the Nazi movement demanded, and it was a blind loyalty that it received from both the SS and the German people. The SS, shrouding itself in medieval initiation rites, oaths, and ceremonies and publicly displaying itself as units of interchangeable black-uniformed components of racial superiority, epitomized the loyalty that was blind to the meaning of its own actions as murder.

It is easy to imagine that when Arendt subtitled her book on the Eichmann trial "A Report on the Banality of Evil" she was using the term *banality* to announce her entrance on the world stage as a kind of modern Cassandra prophesying a future that will be overrun by bloody genocide. But when Arendt calls Eichmann *the banality of evil* she is referring to the blindness that characterized his life as a defendant in the courtroom, as an escaped murderer in Buenos Aires, as a murderous SS officer before that, and, as far as anyone can determine, that characterized his life at every point right up to its last moments. In a sense, Arendt knew what she would see in Jerusalem before she saw it: Eichmann as the icon of the SS, knowing that the SS itself was an icon for the delirium of blind loyalty.

It is doubtful, however, that Arendt knew that what she would hear from Eichmann was the banal evil of substituting blind loyalty for thinking. The term *banal,* as Young-Bruehl points out, did not mean *commonly occurring* to Arendt, but rather meant *commonplace.*[27] In other words, Arendt did not mean that either evil was banal or that the Final Solution was just one more of the banal evils that afflicts humankind; she meant rather that Eichmann, like every human being, possessed the commonplace ability to see himself by thinking about the meaning of who he is. But he was also uncommon in that by not thinking about who he is, he had crossed from the kind of world in which humans usually live to participate in another kind of world that was organized around an axis of murder.

There is nothing in Arendt's work to suggest that she believed that that kind of world, like a common occurrence, would ever appear again. But she knew that if it had appeared once because of the failure of the commonplace capacity of humans to think, then once was enough to question whether thinking can lead us beyond the delirium of a blind loyalty to something we believe what is real about our experience of ourselves and our world. What Arendt heard from Eichmann could never answer the question, but only pose it. From what she heard, Eichmann was "a textbook case of bad faith, of lying self-deception, combined with outrageous stupidity." It is the latter that receives

Arendt's attention, marking him as a "clown."[28] His "outrageous stupidity" was clownish, rather than the absence of intelligence. A better metaphor to describe him, however, because of the association of clown with someone in a mask performing a role, would have been "idiot" in the Dosteyevskian and later Sartrean sense of the term.

Years before the trial Arendt had written that modern religious beliefs cannot be divorced from being put to the test in the modern world, which is a world so suffused with the scientific philosophy of doubting that even the most commonplace things are never what they appear to be. The modern religious believer in a world of wondrous things that have been ordained to be as they are cannot escape confronting that doubt. In this context Arendt observed that "[i]t is noteworthy that the great writer who presented to us in so many figures the modern religious tension between belief and doubt could show a figure of true faith only in the character of *The Idiot*. Modern religious man belongs in the same secular world as his atheistic opponent precisely because he is no 'idiot' in it. The modern believer who cannot bear the tension between doubt and belief will immediately lose the integrity and the profundity of his belief."[29] Eichmann's beliefs as a *Gottglaubiger* were not the beliefs of a religious man who, in the modern world, must bear the tension of doubt. They were beliefs bereft of doubt: the faith of an *idiot*.

Both the idiot and the clown in their respective roles present an innocence easily confused with stupidity but actually is expressive of a powerful loyalty to the world as it gives itself to them. The world as it appears cannot be a deception. Their faith precludes seeing the world in an original way, since they know with certainty that the world is the same for everyone upon whom they depend in their lives. And because everyone they depend on must know the world in the same way they do, nobody in the world would want to deceive them. Their innocence is a lack of self-consciousness, absent because they feel no need to make something different out of themselves or the world that situates them than has already been given. Both the idiot and clown do not insert the tension of doubt into their beliefs because they do not believe they believe—they believe they know. Eichmann the clown was addicted to speaking in clichés, which is the equivalent of not performing the one act that humans can perform to cast doubt on what they believe they know: the act of *thinking*. "The longer one listened to [Eichmann], the more obvious it became that his inability to speak was closely connected with an inability to *think,* namely, to think from the standpoint of somebody else."[30]

On the face of it, to conclude that Eichmann was unable to think "from the standpoint of somebody else" is a strange way to describe Eichmann's failure to think. Arendt, who was not a Kantian moralist, was not referring to Eichmann's failure to live up to Kant's categorical imperative that requires thinking about others' choices as if they were one's own before choosing one's own actions. Neither could she have meant that Eichmann's failure to think from the standpoint of somebody else referred to his addiction to speaking in clichés.

It is virtually a sociological truism that the cliché, in the sense of both a shared and trite stereotypical expression, is essential for humans to perform tasks jointly with others. Can we conceive of what Berger and Luckmann call "a collection of reciprocally typified actions" that together constitute institutionalized behavior without the cliché? Isn't it the interacting of individuals sharing clichés that makes it possible "that each will be able to predict the other's actions?" And isn't it the shared cliché that allows people to think "from the standpoint of somebody else" so that "[t]he 'There he goes again' becomes a 'There *we* go again.'" And finally, isn't it the shared cliché that "relieves both individuals of a considerable amount of tension. They save time and effort, not only in whatever external tasks they might be engaged in separately or jointly, but in terms of their respective psychological economies?"[31] Speaking in clichés can underwrite the delirium of blind loyalty because it underwrites thinking from the standpoint of other people. But if it does, it is because it substitutes for *reflexive* thinking; i.e., thinking in which the "somebody else" is the self itself in the solitary dialogue it conducts with itself. This is what Arendt seems to have meant by describing Eichmann as a clown who is unable to think.

Through the phrase *standpoint of somebody else,* Arendt poses the question of whether reflexive thinking can insert the tension of doubt into the self's certainty about the meaning of itself that it derives from being blindly loyal to some belief. The answer does not become clear until she turns to a critique of Kant in *The Life of the Mind,* years after she wrote about Eichmann. The Kant in whom Arendt is interested, she tells us, is "not the Kant of the *Critique of Pure Reason* . . . but Kant in his pre-critical writings, where he quite freely admits that 'it was [his] fate to fall in love with metaphysics' but also speaks of its 'bottomless abyss,' its 'slippery ground,' its utopian 'land of milk and honey' (*Schlaraffenland*) where the 'dreamers of reason' dwell as though in an 'airship' so that 'there exists no folly which could not be brought to agree with a groundless wisdom.'"[32]

Kant, of course, did not find asking metaphysical questions about God, determinism, and life-after-death meaningless; rather, they dealt with matters that were unknowable and hence belonged to the region of faith. They were, as Arendt reads Kant, "matters that were not given to sense-perception and that their understanding transcended common-sense reasoning, which springs from common-sense experience and can be validated by empirical tests and means."[33] Ultimate questions about God and immortality fall into a region of faith and as such, Kant, in Arendt's terms, had "discovered the 'scandal of reason,' that is, the fact that our mind is not capable of certain and verifiable knowledge regarding matters and questions that it nevertheless cannot help thinking about."[34]

Arendt is concerned with the same problem as Kant: to liberate knowledge of the self from the grasp of the scandal of reason, without treating it as if it were no more than another object in nature. As far as Kant was concerned, we cannot identify knowledge about the self with knowledge about objects in the world because the self cannot be known as if it were a piece of the world rather than the transcendental foundation of knowledge about the world. Nevertheless, knowledge about the self must be true knowledge in the same sense as that disclosed by reasoning about the truth of the world's objects: if we are to say we have knowledge of the self, we must be able to know the laws to which the particular actions of every visible object in the world must conform.

Kant finds these laws constitutive of knowledge of the self by arguing that self is a free agent whose faculty of the will has priority over its faculty of reasoning. Reason discloses the laws by which the free self acts because it can will itself to act in accord with the categorical imperative that is a law, exactly like the laws of nature,[35] that we are obliged to live under as moral agents. As do others, Arendt in her own terms makes it clear that she regards Kant's proof of freedom as irremediably flawed:

This solution, pitting the dictate of the will against the understanding of reason, is ingenious enough and may even suffice to establish a moral law whose logical consistency is in no way inferior to natural laws. But it does little to eliminate the greatest and most dangerous difficulty, namely, that thought itself, in its theoretical as well as its pre-theoretical form, makes freedom disappear—quite apart from the fact that it must appear strange indeed that the faculty of the will whose essential activity consists in dictate and command should be the harborer of freedom.[36]

What Kant had failed to realize was that between the region of empirical knowledge and the region of faith in the existence of what is invisible lies a region of empirical knowledge about what is invisible—the region of the meaning of things that inscribes itself in speech and actions open to observation. He had failed to realize that it is knowing the meaning of things that appear to us, including the self to itself, that is what prompts thinking. "To . . . put it in a nutshell," states Arendt, *"the need of reason is not inspired by the quest for truth but by the quest for meaning. And truth and meaning are not the same.* The basic fallacy, taking precedence over all specific metaphysical fallacies, is to interpret meaning on the model of truth."[37]

Arendt is reversing the precedence of truth over meaning that the West has regarded as authoritatively defining the idea of knowing something since Plato represented it in his parable of the cave. It is only in terms of this reversal that we can establish the starting point for disclosing, by thinking toward ourselves, not the *truth* but the *truthfulness* of what is real about the self by revealing our relationship to the world. The starting point for this disclosure is not the lawfulness of the world to which the self must conform if it is to be true to its being as a reasoning being, but the experience of being in the world.

By reversing the precedence of truth over meaning, Arendt puts at stake translating the experience *Who am I?* into the question *What am I?* that appeals for its answer to a truth more real than the experience itself. Arendt's reversal, meaning over truth, assumes the reality of the experience of questioning *who I am* over a truth that seeks to defuse the explosiveness of the question by seeking to answer it before it can be asked. To make the self's experience and not the truth of the world the starting point for the self's thinking toward itself radically subverts what is given to an individual as the truth of his identity. Just *how* radical can be gauged from Arendt's reply to Gershom Scholem's biting criticism of her authorship of *Eichmann in Jerusalem.*

〜 **2** 〜

Of all of Arendt's critics, it was Gershom Scholem who understood that in *Eichmann in Jerusalem* she was trying to answer not only the question *Who is Eichmann?* but also *Who am I as a Jew?* It was the basis for his abhorrence of the book as well as for ending his long friendship with her. In a letter to Arendt, published widely in 1963 in both Europe and the United States along with her response, Scholem delivered what must have been for Arendt the most cutting attack of all. He first charges Arendt with having little knowledge about her own people despite having written a book that takes up the unavoidable question of "the Jews and their bearing in the days of the catastrophe."[38] It is true that Arendt devotes almost no space at all in the book to Judaism and the Jewish people, and devotes only a few sketchy pages to the "bearing of the Jews" during the Final Solution on the relationship between the Jewish leadership and the Nazis. Scholem's charge, however, is only a preface to stating what Arendt's ignorance about the Jewish people reveals about herself: "In the Jewish tradition there is a concept, hard to define and yet concrete enough, which we know as *Ahabath Israel:* 'Love of the Jewish people.'. . . In you dear Hannah, as in so many intellectuals who came from the German Left, I find little trace of this."[39]

Scholem's letter pivots on this charge, assembling a litany of evidence to support it: when addressing the question of "why did [Jews] allow themselves to be slaughtered?," Arendt maliciously speaks only of "the *weakness* of the Jewish stance in the world" that produces a "sensation of bitterness and shame"[40]; the tone of her book is one of "flippancy" bereft of "*Herzenstakt*"[41]; in place of "balanced judgment" of the decisions that the Jewish leadership had been forced to make in the ghettoes and elsewhere, she engaged in "a kind of demagogic will-to-overstatement"[42] that implied that the Jews had "collaborated in their own genocide."[43] Scholem's charge that Arendt shows little love for the Jewish people charges her not only with the heinous crime of disloyalty to the people to whom she belongs, but because Scholem regards her "wholly as a daughter of our people and in no other way,"[44] it charges her with the equally heinous crime of cursing herself as a Jew.

Responding to Scholem, Arendt first affirms that yes, she is indeed a daughter of "our people," but that this is not the totality of how she experiences who she is and therefore it is not the total way in which she can be regarded:

> The truth is I have never pretended to be anything else or to be in any way other than I am, and I have never even felt tempted in that direction. . . . I have always regarded my Jewishness as one of the indisputable factual data of my life, and I have never had the wish to change or disclaim facts of this kind.[45]

We have no record of Scholem's response to this, but he must have read it as an outrageous affirmation that Arendt had no love for the Jews. To know herself as a Jew simply because of the "fact" that she was born a Jew—a fact she could readily equate, no less, with the fact that she had been born a woman rather than a man, or born a certain size or a with a certain color of hair, etc.—would be to undermine her very identity as a Jew. Yet it is precisely this kind of subversion that Arendt conveys with the anecdote she tells as part of her response to Scholem's charge that she lacks love for the Jews:

> [L]et me tell you of a conversation I had in Israel with a prominent political personality who was defending the—in my opinion disastrous—non-separation of religion and state in Israel. What he said—I am not sure of the exact words anymore—ran something like this: You will understand that, as a Socialist, I, of course do not believe in God; I believe in the Jewish people. I found this a shocking statement and being too shocked, I did not reply at the time. But I could have answered: the greatness of this people was once that it believed in God, and believed in Him in such a way that its trust and love towards Him was greater than its fear. And now this people believes only in itself? What good can come out of that?—Well, in this sense I do not "love" the Jews, nor do I believe in them; I merely belong to them as a matter of course, beyond dispute or argument.[46]

It is not hard to imagine Scholem being so shocked by Arendt's discounting the "good" that comes from Jews believing in themselves as to conclude that he was listening to a Jew who hated herself as a Jew. It would not be a matter simply of Arendt failing to see that Jews cannot expect anyone else to believe in them except themselves; it would be a matter of a far more profound failing. For Scholem, only self-hate could prevent Jews from knowing that the communal origins of individual Jews are the very root that nourishes and supports their identities as individuals. Being born into the history of the Jews legitimates their identity as individuals. Self-love flows from the community to the individual, leaving individuals with no choice but to love and believe in the people they were born into if they are to love and believe in their own being. It is precisely this which Arendt refuses when she tells Scholem: "[T]he only kind of love I know of and believe in is the love of persons. . . . [L]ove of the Jews would appear to me, since I am myself Jewish, as something rather suspect. I cannot love myself or anything which I know is part and parcel of my own person."[47]

Considering her reply to Scholem as a whole, Arendt is neither denying nor refuting that she is a Jew. She is, however, expressing what it means to take one's experience as the starting point for thinking toward the self as a quest for its meaning, not its truth. On this basis, Arendt can be called an existentialist thinker and while this is not off-target, it does not hit the center of her thought. Her existential connection lies in defining identity as always carrying the burden of doubt, but the direction in which she develops this is Arendt's thought alone.

Arendt indicates her existential connection with her interest in Kierkegaard's paradox that defines the experience of being an individual. Arendt wrote about Kierkegaard as early as 1932, stating that: "Kierkegaard speaks with a contemporary voice; he speaks for an entire generation . . .," the generation of "the post [World War I] years, which brought a willingness to tear down outmoded intellectual structures. . . ."[48] Arendt did not mean to dismiss Kierkegaard as simply a response to a specific historical moment of postwar disillusionment and despair. She was interested in Kierkegaard because his work also represented his own "concrete self [that] succumbs to a cruel psychological addiction to reflection. Taking one's own possibilities seriously is what gives rise to this compulsive reflection. . . ."[49] This marked his work—as her own was to become—as a "revolt of a philosopher against philosophy . . .,"[50] which was ironically to become the foundation for what is sometimes called *existential philosophy*.

Kierkegaard's serious reflections on his own possibilities take as their starting point what it means to say that we experience ourselves as *individuals* to whom possibilities can be attributed. His revolt against philosophy opens the question of how individuals experience being an individual that is foreclosed by an answer that displaces experience with general principles that explain it. Put in terms of our modern preoccupation with achieving a personal identity, Kierkegaard's revolutionary shift in starting point reaches into our own age by rebelling against what Barrett has called "a gap . . . between theory and life" created because "[y]ou entertain and support in argument an intellectual position that you could not possibly live."[51] Kierkegaard would agree with Arendt that a personal identity is the basis for human possibility but, as Arendt does, would refuse to identify the beginning of human possibility with the achievement of identity ordained by a developmental process. For Kierkegaard and Arendt, *identity* is the condition for being a human who exists in time as *possibility*. Serious reflection by an individual on his own possibilities, however, must question the coherency of his own experience of who he is as possibility. It is when this question is posed seriously that the experience of being an individual emerges as the paradox Kierkegaard first made visible in a serious way.

Kierkegaard's paradox can be viewed in relief against his polemic with Hegel. Arendt reads "Kierkegaard's polemic against Hegel . . . not so much [as] a critique of one specific philosopher as it is a rejection of philosophy as such. In Kierkegaard's view, philosophy is so caught up in its own systematics that it forgets and loses sight of the actual self of the philosophizing subject: it never touches the 'individual' in his concrete 'existence.'"[52] It is, Arendt states, "[a]gainst the Hegelian doctrine of thesis, antithesis, and synthesis Kierkegaard sets the fundamental paradoxicality of Christian existence: to be an individual—insofar as one stands alone before God (or death)—and yet no longer to have a self—insofar as this self as an individual is nothing before God if its existence is denied."[53]

What compels Kierkegaard's self-reflection is the question of how he can stand before God simultaneously affirming and denying the certainty that he experiences himself as an individual living a uniquely concrete existence. The individual standing before God simultaneously "renounces his self, his individuality, his worldly possibilities, over against which—and from without, as it were—stands the inexorable reality of God. From its very beginnings, his life is not determined by his own desires, his own possibilities; it is only a consequence, a consequence of being determined by God."[54]

To exist as an individual means being unable to escape the certainty of experiencing living at a specific time and place as someone who, as Barrett puts it in a discussion of Kierkegaard's work, "is possessed by self-concern and who makes decisions about himself and his life. Nor are these decisions merely peripheral; on the contrary, they can enter into the very substance of that person's life and make it what it is."[55] Because the act of deciding is either a self-conscious act—a self-conscious invocation of one's will, as it were—or it is not at all an act of deciding, it is always accompanied by the experience of other possibilities. In the light of where we stand in the world, we know that the "substance of our life" was shaped by decisions we never made and by the outcomes we could not control for decisions we did make and will probably not be able to control for decisions we will make in the future. While we are certain of our existence, we are equally certain that we do not exist as the master of the beings who populate the world, able to make the world, as Arendt puts it, "lose its contingent character which is to say its character of reality" so that "it would no longer appear to man as a world given, but as one created by him."[56] It is as if the experience of being a concrete individual, though unable to escape itself at the same time renounces itself in the presence of the inexorable reality of God.

Arendt's work shadows the Kierkegaardian paradox that Cumming notes is at the heart of existential thought: "[I]n existentialism the 'actual' is handled in terms of its relation to its opposite, the 'possible.'"[57] Arendt reads Kierkegaard turning this against Hegel:

> Against Hegel's system, which presumed to comprehend and explain the "whole," Kierkegaard set the "individual," the single human being, for whom there is neither place nor meaning in a totality controlled by the world spirit. Kierkegaard's point of departure is the individual's sense of being lost in a world otherwise totally explained. The individual stands in constant contradiction to this explained world because his "existence," that is, the very fact of his altogether arbitrary existing (that I am *I* and no one else and that I *am* rather than not am) cannot be foreseen by reason nor resolved by it into something purely thinkable.[58]

The "I am I" and the "I am rather than not am" are not thoughts about who I am, except in the most vacuous sense; they are experiences that I am never without that never cease to inform me that I exist in the singular sense, but which I can neither reason nor think about.

Arendt follows Kierkegaard's paradox into the modern scene: "The situation today is this: The most varied and heterogeneous schools of thought look to Kierkegaard as a prime authority; they all meet on the ambiguous ground of radical skepticism, if, indeed, one can still use that pallid, now almost meaningless term to describe an attitude of despair toward one's own existence and the basic principles of one's own scientific or scholarly field."[59] And "despair," we should point out, is the privileged emotion Kierkegaard willed to existential philosophy by which humans become present to themselves[60] as the producers of the principles that, while giving meaning to the world, can neither explain nor account for those who produce them.

Existential thought, the legatee of Kierkegaard, unravels "the ancient tie between Being and thought that had always guaranteed man his home in the world. . . ."[61] What is unraveled is the image human beings have of themselves as simultaneously being subjects who think about the processes that govern the world, and objects who are part of the world commanded by those processes. This image confronts the many modern scientific psychologists dedicated to exorcising the infamous "ghost in the machine" with an aporia. Rather than the ghost being banished, its presence is felt more keenly than ever by scientific thinkers devoted to exorcising thinking itself. For Kierkegaard, because no one can think past this kind of aporia, thinking must be humbled. Arendt, for whom thinking has a certain power in that it opposes the banality of evil, nevertheless occupies Kierkegaard's starting point that humbles thinking. Thinking must be humble because humans, despite being existing beings who think, are beings whose experience of existing escapes thought. A living, experiencing *I* cannot emerge from thought.

Arendt's paradox is nevertheless not Kierkegaard's and although, as she notes, "[m]odern existential philosophy begins with Kierkegaard" so that "[t]here is no single existential philosopher who does not show evidence of his influence,"[62] her paradox is also not that of modern existential thinkers. The difference appears as a response to a question she herself poses: *What makes us think?* The question, as odd as it may appear at first glance, frames her choice of the defining incident in Sartre's novel, *Nausea,* to mark the difference.

Arendt chooses Sartre's *Nausea* because in two respects she and Sartre occupy the same starting point. Arendt's *The Life of the Mind* and Sartre's *Being and Nothingness,* his formal elaboration of the philosophical underpinnings of his novel, begin in strikingly similar terms. Arendt begins, after her introduction, with the statement that "[t]he world men are born into contains many things, natural and artificial, living and dead, transient and sempiternal, all of which have in common that they *appear* and hence are meant to be seen, heard, touched, tasted, and smelled, to be perceived by sentient creatures endowed with the appropriate sense organs. . . . In this world which we enter appearing from a nowhere, and from which we disappear into a nowhere, *Being and Appearing coincide.*"[63]

The coincidence between *being* and *appearing* is also the opening theme in Sartre's *Being and Nothingness:* "[I]f once we get away from what Nietzsche called 'the illusion of worlds behind the scene,' and if we no longer believe in the being-behind-the-appearance, then the appearance becomes full positivity; its essence is an 'appearing' which is no longer opposed to being but on the contrary is the measure of it. For the being of an existent is exactly what it *appears.* Thus we arrive at the idea of the *phenomenon* such as we can find, for example, in the 'phenomenology' of Husserl or Heidegger."[64]

And the idea of the phenomenon contains for both Arendt and Sartre, as Arendt puts it, "Husserl's basic and greatest discovery . . . the intentionality of all acts of consciousness, that is, the fact that no subjective act is ever without an object. . . . Objectivity is built into the very subjectivity of consciousness by virtue of intentionality. Conversely, and with the same justness, one may speak of the intentionality of appearances and their built-in subjectivity. All objects because they appear indicate a subject, and just as every subjective act has its intentional object, so every appearing object has its intentional subject."[65] Sartre puts it more succinctly: The phenomenon is "the relative absolute. Relative the phenomenon remains, for 'to appear' supposes in essence somebody to whom to appear."[66]

The idea that nothing and nobody appears in this world whose being does not suppose a spectator includes, for both Arendt and Sartre, the appearance of the self to itself. But neither Arendt nor Sartre takes this as a starting point for following Husserl and Heidegger down the path of attempting to establish through a description of individuals' experiences the necessary truth of the being of human beings. In this respect, Husserl's famous call "to the things themselves," as Arendt put it, "is . . . a magic formula. . . . If we could still achieve anything by magic—in an age whose only good is that all magic fails in it—we would indeed have to begin with the smallest and seemingly most modest of things, with unpretentious 'little things,' with unpretentious words."[67]

Both Arendt and Sartre from their overlapping starting points move toward understanding the meaning that objects that appear, including the self, have for individuals who act in situations of ordinary social life. Each wants to change social life by changing the actions of individuals who speak and think about what they say to both themselves and others. Each wants to establish as the starting point for those changes the human experience of the visible world that appears to them, in opposition to the starting point that holds modernity in an iron grip: That the reality of what appears to the self is invisible until the self forces it to show itself.

Arendt and Sartre, however, move from their overlapping starting points in radically divergent directions. For Arendt, Sartre's *Nausea* underscores their divergence, which is undoubtedly one reason she makes the eccentric judgment that it is "by far the most important of his philosophical works."[68]

The incident in Sartre's novel that is important to her is the one where, as she paraphrases it, "the hero of the novel [Roquentin], looking at the root of a chestnut tree, has been suddenly overcome by 'what to *exist* meant. . . .' The reaction of Sartre's hero is not admiration, and not even wonder, but 'nausea at the opaqueness of sheer existence, at the naked thereness of the factually given, which indeed, no thought has ever succeeded in reaching, let alone illuminating and making transparent. . . .'"[69] What is important to Arendt is not Sartre's hero Roquentin's nausea as such, which of course no one other than Roquentin may ever feel toward the root of a chestnut tree. When one appeals to the experience of individuals as the starting point for defining what it means to be an individual, it is no longer a question of testing a hypothesis by counting the number of individuals who may or may not become nauseous in front of the roots of chestnut trees. It is rather a question of what Roquentin's singular reaction of nausea illuminates about the relations that individuals universally have to themselves and the world as individuals, whether or not they have ever seen a chestnut tree. It is precisely in such terms that Freud, for example, universalized the meaning of the distinctly singular dreams that people have as the starting point for a body of work that helped shape an entire century's thinking.

Sartre presents Roquentin's revelation at the chestnut tree as the culmination of a kind of Kierkegaardian, obsessive self-reflection whereby Roquentin has liberated himself from relating to the appearance of the life that he had been living as the only possibility for his existence. He had come to see that his life had been unfolding like a story you can only tell from the outside when you reach an ending that allows you to look back on it and make something of it; but what you make of it from the outside when you tell it is never what you lived. Of course, there are plenty of stories that are told about his life—religious, philosophical, scientific, political—as if they told the truth of what he was living, but they were not stories he could ever experience as his own. As Iris Murdoch put it: "Roquentin visits the picture gallery, and looks at the self-satisfied faces of the bourgeoisie. . . . Their lives had a real given meaning, or so they imagined; and here they are, with all that added sense of necessity with which the painter's thought can endow them. Roquentin's recent experience has given him a special sense of the bad faith of these attempts to clothe the nakedness of existence with such trimmings of meaning."[70]

"Bad faith" is Sartre's way of characterizing our attempts to avoid disclosing to ourselves the paradoxical experience of our individuality whose marker is the thinly veiled anguish that never ceases to haunt our lives. "Kierkegaard is right," Sartre tells us in *Being and Nothingness,* "anguish is distinguished from fear in that fear is fear of beings in the world, whereas anguish is anguish before myself."[71] Sartre's *bad faith* is a belief about ourselves that functions to deceive us about the truth of our disjointed relationship with ourselves. To put it another way, *bad faith* is a "cover story," to use Fingarette's term,[72] that we tell ourselves about the *giveness* of our identities to account for our anguish as a struggle to become who we know we are because it is who we are told we should be.

But at the chestnut tree Roquentin became conscious of experiencing himself situated in the world as it is, not in terms of the meaning that others presented as its truth. In the presence of the world as it is, Roquentin stood in the presence of himself as anguish no longer varnished by the stories that others told to explain his experiences to him. That Roquentin could no longer think about the meaning of himself in terms that others had created is Sartre's way of stating that God is dead and that we can no longer take refuge in those processes that presumed to state the *truth* about the order and meaning of the world and our lives within it.

Arendt is not taking issue with Sartre's depiction of Roquentin's project of liberating himself from such systems of thought; what she takes exception to is Sartre's representation of Roquentin's experience of standing in the presence of the world as it is, unsupported by the deceptions of bad faith. As Arendt puts it, quoting Sartre, Roquentin was left experiencing a world that was a "completely meaningless thereness that makes the hero shout: 'Filth! what rotten filth! . . . but it held fast and there was so much, tons and tons of existence, endless.'"[73] Roquentin's nausea is a vertiginous nausea, not because there is too much of that "endless" stuff that makes up the world, but because there is too little of himself. If what we truly desired were objects in the world, Roquentin might be depicted as experiencing a certain giddiness in the face of a plenitude of possibilities rather than nausea as if tons of filth were burying his possibilities.

For Sartre, behind every object we desire in the world is ourself as the object of our desire. In the spirit of Kierkegaard, existence, for Sartre in *Nausea,* is a movement forward that we make with a staggering gait, falling into the emptiness of ourselves only to recover with the anguished desire to fill that emptiness with ourselves. Bereft of his own bad faith, Roquentin stands in the presence of a *meaningless thereness* as the unthinkable nothingness Sartre chose to call "freedom" in *Being and Nothingness.* Freedom for Sartre, in *Being and Nothingness,* "is the freedom of choosing but not the freedom of not choosing,"[74] and what freedom must choose is an identity it desires to be even though it can never be that identity. Humans for Sartre are "always engaged . . . as a choice in the making."[75] The paradoxical relationship of the individual to himself is the inverse reflection of the dense, unfeeling positivity of the absurd plenitude of meaningless stuff that makes up the world—like the root of a chestnut tree.

For Arendt, Sartre is flat-out wrong in depicting individuals' experiencing the world, through the transparency of their paradoxical relationship to themselves, to be a *meaningless thereness.* But how could

Sartre not depict the world in these terms after depicting in *Nausea* that the self's quest for the meaning of itself is exhausted by bad faith, and therefore bad faith exhausts human possibility? For Roquentin, fully aware that he is in bad faith, no meaning of himself can ever again be meaningful, since it is impossible for him to choose a meaning of himself because there is nothing to support his choice—neither himself nor the world, but only bad faith.

In fact, Iris Murdoch, in a shrewd observation on Sartre's ending his novel by having Roquentin, in a cafe, caught up in the vivifying sensations of listening to a recording of his favorite tune, "Some of These Days," calls him "a Platonist by nature. His ideal mode of being, to which he often recurs in thought, is that of a mathematical figure— pure, clear, necessary and non-existent."[76] Nonexistent because no human being can exist as an abstract form, only as a concrete individual who experiences a world in which things have their reality in their density and not in their form. If the only thing that makes us think is our desire to reclaim our will to choose a meaning for ourselves from our own bad faith, then the satisfaction of that desire means willing ourselves part of an absurd, meaningless world that can never affirm that the meaning of ourselves that we have willed for ourselves is meaningful. We can will our choice of ourselves to have meaning only by returning to a bad faith that paradoxically is no longer possible once it is blown as a cover story.

Arendt, while following the trail from Kierkegaard's starting point to the dilemma that we are dependent on others who populate the world for our identity, but who, because they are *other,* can never affirm the identity we choose to be, supplies an answer to the question *What makes us think?* that refuses Sartre's characterization of the world as a meaningless, self-negating horror. What makes us think is what has always made us think: the experience of the world as a wonder. Experiencing wonder at the world is for Arendt one of the "pre-philosophic assumptions which became so very important for the history of metaphysics,"[77] setting philosophical thinking on its quest to dispel the mystery of the world. "[T]he origin of philosophy is Wonder . . .," Arendt states,[78] pointing out that "what sets men wondering is something familiar and yet normally invisible, and something men are forced to *admire*. The wonder that is the starting point for thinking is neither puzzlement nor surprise nor perplexity; it is an *admiring* wonder."[79]

Arendt's answer is a refusal to follow Sartre from the explosive doubt of Roquentin about the meaning of himself to an equally explosive doubt about the possibility of a meaningful world; a world whose reality does not disappear but dissolves in the self-consciousness of a subject who has discovered that it has no meaning as reality outside of his own intentional acts. This is not a world at all as Roquentin discovered, but a particular kind of horror: a horror that dissolves the conviction of the subject himself that he himself is real.

Arendt, refusing to follow Sartre, turns to Merleau-Ponty whose project, similar to her own, was to rethink, as he himself put it, "reflection . . . carried away and transplanted in an impregnable subjectivity, as yet untouched by being and time." This is a "very ingenuous, or at least it is an incomplete form of reflection which loses sight of its own beginning . . . . [I]t has to recognize, as having priority over its own operations, the world which is given to the subject, because the subject is given to himself. The real has to be described, not constructed or formed."[80]

~ 3 ~

Through Merleau-Ponty Arendt states another reversal of the precedence of truth over meaning. This time it is to return us to the world while still insisting that meaning and truth are not the same. Now, while meaning still has precedence over truth, something has precedence over meaning: the appearance of the world that is not the same as its meaning. Before something appears meaningful there must be, as Arendt puts it, "our 'perceptual faith,' as Merleau-Ponty has called it, our certainty that what we perceive has an existence independent of the act of perceiving [that] depends entirely on the object's also appearing as such to others and being acknowledged by them. Without this tacit acknowledgement by others we would not even be able to put faith in the way we appear to ourselves."[81] Arendt is appealing to Merleau-Ponty's notion of *perceptual faith* to provide a ground of unshakable certainty that whatever doubts the self must inevitably have about its identity, there is an unshakable reality to itself beneath its meaningful appearance that cannot be doubted.

Arendt does not explicate Merleau-Ponty's notion of *perceptual faith,* but Whiteside does: "Only phenomenology gives an account of the fundamental layer of experience called 'perception.' . . . It is in the nature of our perceptual relationship to things, contends Merleau-Ponty, that we see them through successive profiles. Perception is inherently incomplete. It is not, for all that, inherently uncertain." We are certain that we are seeing more of things than we literally see because "[a] profile refers beyond itself to the structure of the whole. . . ." The certainty of this makes meaning possible: "It is appropriate to refer to 'meaning' here (if only 'nascent' or 'imminent') because the functions of reference, demarcation, and differentiation, which we normally ascribe to precise, conceptual definition, are already prefigured in our spontaneous perception."[82]

In other words, as intentional consciousness we are able to constitute the meaning of objects only because we first perceive them as whole objects, demarcated outside our own boundaries. It is our sense that the ground for meaning is *difference* that prefigures the meanings we constitute. The concept of *prefigured* does not refer to anything that causally determines meaning; meaning is not a secondary effect of the way putative prefiguring processes operate. The concept refers to what is made manifest in the experience of meaning that defines what it is to be a being with human experiences.

Arendt's approach to defining exactly what is manifested in meaning is different than Merleau-Ponty's. But when she states, as she did in *The Human Condition,* that "nothing entitles us to assume that man has a nature or essence in the same sense as other things" and to attempt to define such an essence "would be like jumping over our own shadows,"[83] she is sharing with Merleau-Ponty the position that because humans cannot be said to have a human nature does not mean that they are not part of the world of natural creatures. For Arendt, we are similar to all other creatures because "[s]een from the perspective of the world, every creature born into it arrives well equipped to deal with a world in which Being and Appearing coincide; they are fit for worldly existence."[84] This fitness is what Arendt calls "an urge toward self-display. . . ."[85]

Arendt is very clear that with this notion she means to reverse "the old prejudice of Being's supremacy over appearance"[86] to which the human sciences stubbornly cling in their claims to be authentic sciences. "Could it not be" she asks again rhetorically, "that appearances are not there for the sake of the life process but, on the contrary, that the life process is there for the sake of appearances? Since we live in an *appearing* world, is it not more plausible that the relevant and the meaningful in this world of ours should be located precisely on the surface?"[87] In other words, put in a more declarative language, the identity we reflect on that we must live, if we are to live vivifying relationships with others, does not represent some truth we are told lies hidden at the core of our being waiting to express itself, but represents the way we display ourselves to be seen and related to by others.

To explicate this, Arendt turns to the work of "the Swiss zoologist and biologist Adolf Portmann [who] has shown that the facts themselves speak a very different language from the simplistic functional hypothesis that holds that appearances in living beings serve merely the twofold purpose of self-preservation and preservation of the species." She then proceeds to quote Portmann: "Prior to all functions for the purpose of preservation of the individual and the species . . . [*sic*] we find the simple fact of appearing as self-display *that makes these functions meaningful* [Arendt's italics]."[88] What is important to Arendt is that Portmann sets up an opposition between, as she quotes him, "the functional form pure and simple, so much extolled by some as befitting nature" and, as she puts it, Portmann's "'morphology,' a new science that would reverse the priorities: '*Not what something is but how it appears is the research problem* [Arendt's italics].'"[89]

Arendt, of course, is not calling for a biological research program into the human urge for self-display. The actions of all creatures of the same species toward each other are actions governed by rules and mediated by some form of communication. But for no other creature can we say that these rules are located in the language in which they speak and think. Put another way, a world exists for humans to experience because it is a conceptual world organized by rules of language that mandate how things are similar and different from each other. Humans do not live in pairs, or groups, or even in communities, but in cultures that, Geertz points out, must "be treated as significative systems posing expositive questions."[90] Human actions call for an understanding that falls within a region governed, as Ricouer puts it, by "mental life itself, its creative dynamism, which calls for the mediation (of understanding) by 'meanings,' 'values' or 'goals'"[91] because, in Taylor's terms, "an action, feeling or thought is what it is only in virtue of its having a certain meaning; hence the conditions of the intelligibility of the meaning are the conditions of existence for the action, or feeling."[92] The human world of meaning, for Arendt, is founded on "the urge for self-display," but while a foundation is more primary than that which it founds, the term *urge* is left vague precisely because it has no empirical reality outside of the language in which we think and speak that is its manifestation.

To redefine the paradoxical experience of being an individual from the *fact* that we appear to ourselves as meaningful, to a paradox that arises from the meaning of the self as a manifestation of the *urge* to display the self, is to nullify the tendency in existential thought to "almost automatically equate freedom with free will. . . ."[93] By nullifying this equation Arendt is implicitly refusing the notion that the continuity of my identity—referring to the fact when, for instance, I look at childhood photos of myself, no matter how strange I may appear, I always recognize myself—can be accounted for by an ideology of character imprisoning my free will. Arendt follows existential thinking from Kierkegaard by recognizing that the experience of being a continuous identity is not the end-state of a natural process; but neither is it for her an experience that conceals "being" the freedom to will the meaning of the self. The experience of being a continuous identity, rather, is the primordial condition that guarantees that a display of the self will result in a meaningful relation to other human beings.

What is it then that is open to reflexive thinking? A succinct answer is found in Arendt's statement that "[l]iving things make their appearance like actors on a stage set for them."[94] This may be true as we observe all "living things," but the thrust of Arendt's statement is to extend what Merleau-Ponty speaks of as the certainty of humans perceiving the profile of the world as real before they endow it with meaning, to the perception of the world as a stage on which stories are ready to be lived. The idea that humans live stories rather than just tell them means, as Ricouer points out, that we live our lives using "in a meaningful way the entire network of expressions and concepts that are offered to us by natural languages in order to distinguish between *action* and mere physical *movement* and psychophysiological *behavior.* In this way, we understand what is signified by project, aim, means, circumstances and so on. . . . [I]t is the same phronetic understanding which presides over the understanding of action (and of passion) and over that of narrative."[95] Stories do not represent a metaphoric model imposed from the outside to prepare human experience for an ostensibly more profound causal analysis of *process*. They are the form in which a primordial perception of the reality of the world manifests itself in a display of the meaning of the self. What is open to my reflexive thinking is the meaning of myself as a continuous identity necessitated by my having to display myself playing a role in a story that conveys the meaning of who I am.

Following Arendt's thinking in this regard can be facilitated by seeing how it goes beyond David Carr's revision of Husserlian phenomenology. As with Carr, for Arendt consciousness as intentionality toward the meaning of what it is conscious of is structured; and narrative is integral to its structure. Human subjects live in time, "and the experience of time," Carr points out, "is narrative—or more humbly, story and story telling. . . . [N]arrative is our primary (though not our only) way of organizing our experience of time. . . ."[96] It is primary in the sense of both principal and original. The ubiquity of narrative at all levels of human life, Carr argues, expresses neither the need of identifiable story tellers nor anonymous cultural rules to make sense of the world, as if the world is always originally experienced by human beings as chaotic. Narrative "is prefigured in certain features of life, action and communication." In this regard Carr admiringly quotes Barbara Hardy, "who holds that 'narrative, like lyric or dance, is not to be regarded as an aesthetic invention used by artists to control, manipulate, and order experience, but as a primary act of mind transferred from art to life.'"[97] Carr is unequivocally clear about what he is arguing: "[N]arrative form is not a dress which covers something else but the structure inherent in human experience and action,"[98] and "it is the organizing principle not only of experience and actions but of the self who experiences and acts."[99]

To be a self who experiences and acts is, at times, to be an unselfconscious self totally absorbed in experiencing the world toward which actions are directed. But that does not mean that the self who experiences and acts is without an awareness of itself that never leaves it while it lives: That its experiences and actions, directed toward the future, have a past. Without this awareness, which Carr describes as "not only pre-theoretical but also pre-thematic; that is, it is an awareness in which the historical past is involved in ordinary experience even when we are not explicitly thinking about it,"[100] we would be conscious that our actions are directed toward what is immediately present that appears to us, but have no basis for experiencing our actions as anything other than fragmented and disjointed sequences that randomly follow one another.

Carr explicates this by turning to Husserl's account of the experience of listening to a musical melody:

> If consciousness of the past is memory, then we must recognize here, says Husserl, a special sort of memory, whose object is the just-past which attaches itself immediately to the present. Thanks to this sort of memory, I have consciousness not only of the succession of notes which make up the melody, but of the very presentness of the present; to hear the present note sound is to be conscious of its occurring or *taking place*; but its taking place is precisely its taking the place of its predecessor. To be conscious of its occurrence is to be conscious also of the "comet tail" that trails behind it. Husserl's great contribution here lies in his recognition of this peculiar form of memory which he calls primary memory or retention.[101]

But, of course, to be conscious of something taking place in what we experience to be the present is possible not only because of retention of the past, but also because of an expectation of the future, which Husserl calls "protention."[102] As any child can tell us, we read time backward. There is no past except on the horizon of a future end to a story that is eagerly awaited to bring a final order to everything that preceded it. At the same time there is no future except on the horizon of a past that is the progression of scenes that awaits ordering by a future ending. In effect, we can be conscious of something that appears to us whose meaning we intend only if it appears to us as standing out on the double horizons of past and future. It is this that Carr refers to as the prefiguration of narrative inherent in the structure of the intention toward meaning before meaning is intended.

All of this is consistent with Arendt's going a step beyond Merleau-Ponty by appealing to the reality of the world as a stage on which stories are ready to be enacted. What is critical to Arendt as it is to Carr is that the story that conveys the meaning and significance of events is not a function of humans projecting a narrative order on otherwise chaotic events, but is a function of the necessity for events to appear in the form of narratives if they are to appear in any way meaningful to humans.

But Arendt's narrative model of meaning, unlike Carr's, retains its grounding in a radically individualistic phenomenology. Arendt would certainly not disagree with Carr that to understand the temporality of history, as distinct from an individual's experience, requires asking, as Carr does, "[h]ow do we initiate an investigation of social reality, centered on the social group, whose point of departure is neither the phenomenological *I* nor the straightforward treatment of an *it*, an item in the world?"[103] For a species whose members can institute the reality of each other only by speaking about each other, there can be no other reality than one composed of groups, since language is the medium for concepts, making thinking the unique impossible.

But what does it mean to propose, as does Carr, treating "the group not as object but as subject?"[104] Clearly, we talk about groups that way, but Carr is clear that while it is not meaningless to do so, it does not mean that groups are "persons 'writ large.'"[105] Groups are spoken of by their members as a "we subject" because they "are often characterized by an intersubjectivity which is not only successive but also simultaneous and cooperative."[106] In other words, groups function in time to accomplish projects, but the individual members do not necessarily experience their involvement in those projects as if they were experiencing the unfolding of a sequence of musical notes in time that produces a melody. Group projects "are collective endeavors in which individuals work in teams. This means that they not only have a shared objective but also distribute tasks among the individuals who participate. . . . Asked who carried out the action in question, the individual participant would have to answer: 'We did.'"[107]

Carr's point that individuals experience the social reality of groups as the reality of "we subjects" has to be well taken, as well as his point that individuals who are members of a group identify themselves with the group to experience it as an agent whose acts can be told in a story about meaningful motives, purposes, and reasons: "When individual actions are conceived by participants as part of a common project . . . their meaning is derived from the project, which is the undertaking properly speaking of the group and not of the individuals. Whatever the group may be 'in itself,' or to an external observer, for the participants it is postulated as the subject which gives meaning to their behavior, the agent whose action is the overall framework of the subactions they as individuals perform."[108] But Arendt would have to say that Carr does not go far enough, or to put it more forcefully, it is essential to go beyond Carr as careful as he is to warn us not to reify the idea of a *we subject* in such a way as to "submerge or obliterate the plurality of individuals that make it up."[109]

From Arendt's standpoint the problem is that Carr seems to think that social reality—community itself as the reality composed of groups and institutions—is possible only when we can envisage "a form of association in which a genuine group subject is formed."[110] This privileges from suspicion the individual's identification with his group in the name of the possibility of a "genuine group subject" whose actions Carr equates with social reality. In effect, Carr is sanctioning individuals deriving the meaning of themselves from the role they play, along with others, in the story they live about the group's projects. Arendt would have to say that Carr does not go far enough because it is precisely the banal, commonplace identification of individuals with the groups in which they participate and from which, as team members, they derive their identities that defines the possibility of the blind loyalty Arendt calls *the banality of evil*. By the time Arendt stated in *The Life of the Mind* that "[i]f there is anything in thinking that can prevent men from doing evil, it must be some property inherent in the activity itself, regardless of its objects,"[111] she had already indicated that at least one of the properties of thinking is to resist such identifications before they can lead to evil.

Reflexive thinking that withdraws attention from objects in the world is a dialogue conducted with oneself as if one were thinking about the meaning of oneself from the standpoint of someone else. What the quest for meaning uncovers is that an individual's coherent meaning of himself, from the beginning, was always an illusion and would always remain an illusion that is the inexorable experience of the reality of experiencing himself as an individual. Thinking toward the meaning of the self does not separate individuals from acting in groups that make up the reality of the social world. For Arendt, an individual's coherent experience of the meaning of himself never stops depending "upon a world that solidly appears as the location for its own appearance, on fellow creatures [acting in roles] to play with, and on spectators to acknowledge and recognize its existence."[112] What the activity of reflexive thinking does is disclose that doubt is at the heart of whatever coherent identity an individual may seek to derive from identifying with the groups in which he must play a role in order to function as a social being. The activity of thinking, directed toward a quest for the meaning of the self, demarcates the thinking individual from the groups in which he participates that make up social reality. By thinking toward the meaning of itself, the self uncovers itself as a being who can never experience the authentic identity that a social group may proffer to him. The world, made up of groups, is a world that cannot be made into a home. The coherency of identity is a problem without a solution.

Carr understates the problem when he defines it as one in which "life does fall short of art, that it fails to live up to the formal coherence and the clear-cut authorship of some stories. But this is because to live it is to make the constant demand and attempt that it approach that coherence."[113] The basis for the problem of a coherent identity is not an individual aspiring to live his life by an impossible aesthetic standard as if he were the author of a fictional story. The problem arises from the fact that one's own individual history does not begin with one's own beginning; rather, one's own beginning itself has a beginning into which one's own beginning is inserted. In effect, whatever story an individual seeks to live as the meaning of the identity he is displaying, it proves to be a story that is in the middle of a larger story called the history of a group, a society, a nation, and virtually the entire human world. And this story that no individual can escape living, as everyone knows, has no beginning, no end, and no author. Arendt puts it this way:

> The realm of human affairs, strictly speaking, consists of the web of human relationships which exists wherever men live together. The disclosure of the "who" through speech, and the setting of a new beginning through action, always fall into an already existing web where their immediate consequences can be felt. Together they start a new process which eventually emerges as the unique life story of the newcomer, affecting uniquely the life stories of all those with whom he comes into contact. It is because of this already existing web of human relationships, with its innumerable, conflicting wills and intentions, that action almost never achieves its purpose. . . . Although everybody started his life by inserting himself into the human world through action and speech, nobody is the author or producer of his own life story. In other

words, the stories, the results of action and speech, reveal an agent, but this agent is not an author or producer. Somebody began it and is its subject in the twofold sense of the word, namely its actor and sufferer, but nobody is its author.[114]

The coherency of identity is not just an unresolvable problem; identity is what we suffer. The experience of having a coherent identity dependent on the acknowledgement and recognition of others who play different roles is a problem inherent in a pluralistic world of individuals who have different angles of vision on the meaning of what appears to them. No loyalty to a *we subject* with which individuals identify to derive a meaning to themselves can be more than an apparition animated by the suppression of thinking toward the meaning of the self. This includes identifying with the group into which an individual may be born. It is true that to be born a Jew in a world of enemies who will never let you be known except as a disease that must be eradicated means that you have no recourse but not to doubt who you are by thinking. But this would not be a matter of substituting blind loyalty for thinking; it would be a matter of substituting fighting for thinking so that you can return to the possibility of thinking.

In Arendt's work, thinking toward the self encounters a beginning that is as solid and immovable as the fact that one exists as a person; but that beginning is not the meaning of one's identity. What thinking discloses about who one is is that doubt is always at the heart of the meaning of the self from its beginning. And yet the hard fact of one's beginning is critical. Without such a foundation it would be impossible for the self to ever make something new of itself. And here Arendt makes a truly remarkable and original connection: The possibility of the individual making something new of himself out of his beginning is identical to the possibility of human beings conducting a political life that defines the condition for their existence in a world occupied by other beings like themselves. This brings us back to the theme of Arendt's peculiar history, *The Origins of Totalitarianism.* What Arendt has called "the subterranean stream of European history"[115] is precisely the disappearance of "the political" that found its ultimate form in the Nazi movement that crossed the line from the erosion of individuality that preceded it to the destruction of the very idea of the individual.

Notes

1. Quoted in Elisabeth Young-Bruehl, *Hannah Arendt: For Love of the World* (New Haven, CT: Yale University Press, 1982), 329.

2. Hannah Arendt, *Eichmann in Jerusalem: A Report on the Banality of Evil*, rev. ed. (New York: Penguin Books, 1977), 21.

3. Gideon Hausner, "Eichmann and His Trial," *The Saturday Evening Post* (Nov. 1962).

4. Arendt, *Eichmann in Jerusalem*, 21.

5. Hans H. Gerth and C. Wright Mills, eds., *From Max Weber: Essays in Sociology* (Oxford: Oxford University Press, 1946), 215–16.

6. Hannah Arendt, *The Origins of Totalitarianism*, 3d ed. (New York: Harvest/HBJ, 1968), 245.

7. John Pawlikowski, "The Holocaust and Contemporary Christology" in Elisabeth Schussler Fiorenza and David Tracy, eds., *The Holocaust as Interruption* (Edinburgh: T. and T. Clark, 1984), 45.

8. Pawlikowski, "The Holocaust and Contemporary Christology," 45.

9. Arendt, *Eichmann in Jerusalem*, 25.

10. Arendt, *Eichmann in Jerusalem*, 136.

11. Arendt, *Eichmann in Jerusalem*, 136.

12. Arendt, *Eichmann in Jerusalem*, 137.

13. Quoted in William L. Hull, *The Struggle for a Soul* (Garden City, NY: Doubleday, 1963), 149.

14. Arendt, *Eichmann in Jerusalem*, 41–42.

15. Quoted in Peter Padfield, *Himmler: Reichsfuehrer—SS* (New York: Henry Holt, 1990), 182.

16. Arendt, *The Origins of Totalitarianism*, 385.

17. Arendt, *The Origins of Totalitarianism*, 373.

18. Michael Burleigh and Wolfgang Wipperman, *The Racial State: Germany 1933–1945* (Cambridge, UK: Cambridge University Press, 1991), 270–71.

19. Burleigh and Wipperman, *The Racial State*, 273–74.

20. Herbert F. Ziegler, *Nazi Germany's New Aristocracy* (Princeton, NJ: Princeton University Press, 1989), xiv–xv.

21. Quoted in Ziegler, *Nazi Germany's New Aristocracy*, 52.

22. Quoted in Saul Friedlander, *Reflections on Nazism*, tr. Thomas Weyr (New York: Harper and Row, 1984), 102–3.

23. Ernst Klee, Willi Dressen, and Volker Riess, eds., *The Good Old Days: The Holocaust as Seen by Its Perpetrators and Bystanders*, tr. Deborah Burnstone (New York: The Free Press, 1991), 78–79.

24. Klee, Dressen, and Riess, *The Good Old Days,* 63.

25. Padfield, *Himmler,* 139.

26. Quoted in Friedlander, *Reflections on Nazism,* 103.

27. Elisabeth Young-Bruehl, "From the Pariah's Point of View: Reflections on Hannah Arendt's Life and Work," in *Hannah Arendt: The Recovery of the Public World,* ed. Melvyn Hill (New York: St. Martin's Press, 1979), 17.

28. Arendt, *Eichmann in Jerusalem,* 54.

29. Hannah Arendt, *Essays in Understanding: 1930–1945* (New York: Harcourt, Brace, 1994), 370–71.

30. Arendt, *Eichmann in Jerusalem,* 49.

31. Peter L. Berger and Thomas Luckmann, *The Social Construction of Reality* (Garden City, NY: Anchor Books/Doubleday, 1967), 57.

32. Hannah Arendt, *The Life of the Mind,* vol. 1 (New York: Harcourt, Brace, Jovanovitch, 1978), 9.

33. Arendt, *The Life of the Mind,* vol. 1, 13.

34. Arendt, *The Life of the Mind,* vol. 1, 14.

35. J. B. Schneewind, "Autonomy, Obligation, and Virtue: An Overview of Kant's Moral Philosophy," in *The Cambridge Companion to Kant,* ed. Paul Guyer (Cambridge, UK: Cambridge University Press, 1992), 320.

36. Hannah Arendt, *Between Past and Future,* expanded ed. (New York: Penguin Books, 1977), 145.

37. Arendt, *The Life of the Mind,* vol. 1, 15.

38. "Eichmann in Jerusalem: Exchange of Letters Between Gershom Scholem and Hannah Arendt," in *The Jew As Pariah,* ed. Ron Feldman (New York: Grove Press, 1978), 240–41.

39. "Eichmann in Jerusalem: Exchange of Letters," 241.

40. "Eichmann in Jerusalem: Exchange of Letters," 241.

41. "Eichmann in Jerusalem: Exchange of Letters," 242.

42. "Eichmann in Jerusalem: Exchange of Letters," 242–43.

43. "Eichmann in Jerusalem: Exchange of Letters," 242–43.

44. "Eichmann in Jerusalem: Exchange of Letters," 242.

45. "Eichmann in Jerusalem: Exchange of Letters," 246.

46. "Eichmann in Jerusalem: Exchange of Letters," 247.

47. "Eichmann in Jerusalem: Exchange of Letters," 246–47.

48. Arendt, *Essays in Understanding,* 44–45.

49. Arendt, *Essays in Understanding,* 48.

50. Arendt, *Essays in Understanding,* 45.

51. William Barrett, *Death of the Soul: From Descartes to the Computer* (Garden City, NY: Anchor Press/Doubleday, 1986), xiii.

52. Arendt, *Essays in Understanding,* 45.

53. Arendt, *Essays in Understanding,* 46.

54. Arendt, *Essays in Understanding,* 47.

55. Barrett, *Death of the Soul,* 126.

56. Arendt, *Essays in Understanding,* 165.

57. Robert Denoon Cumming, *The Starting Point* (Chicago: University of Chicago Press, 1979), 77.

58. Arendt, *Essays in Understanding,* 173.

59. Arendt, *Essays in Understanding,* 173.

60. Bernard J. Bergen, *Illumination by Darkness* (New York: Peter Lang, 1992), 143.

61. Arendt, *Essays in Understanding,* 164.

62. Arendt, *Essays in Understanding,* 173.

63. Arendt, *The Life of the Mind,* vol. 1, 19.

64. Jean-Paul Sartre, *Being and Nothingness,* tr. Hazel E. Barnes (New York: Washington Square Press/Pocket Books, 1966), 4.

65. Arendt, *The Life of the Mind,* vol. 1, 46.

66. Sartre, *Being and Nothingness,* 4.

67. Arendt, *Essays in Understanding,* 166.

68. Arendt, *The Life of the Mind,* vol. 1, 147.

69. Arendt, *The Life of the Mind,* vol. 1, 147.

70. Iris Murdoch, *Sartre: Romantic Rationalist* (New Haven, CT: Yale University Press, 1953), 2-3.

71. Sartre, *Being and Nothingness,* 39.

72. Bergen, *Illumination by Darkness,* 81.

73. Arendt, *The Life of the Mind,* vol. 1, 147–48.

74. Sartre, *Being and Nothingness,* 618.

75. Sartre, *Being and Nothingness,* 616.

76. Murdoch, *Sartre,* 7.

77. Arendt, *The Life of the Mind,* vol. 1, 143.

78. Arendt, *The Life of the Mind,* vol. 1, 141.

79. Arendt, *The Life of the Mind,* vol. 1, 143.

80. Maurice Merleau-Ponty, "Preface to 'Phenomenology of Perception'," in *Phenomenology and Existentialism,* ed. R. Zaner and D. Ihde (New York: Putnam, 1973), 75.

81. Arendt, *The Life of the Mind,* vol. 1, 46.

82. Kerry H. Whiteside, *Merleau-Ponty and the Foundation of an Existential Politics* (Princeton, NJ: Princeton University Press, 1988), 47.

83. Hannah Arendt, *The Human Condition* (Chicago: University of Chicago Press, 1958), 10.

84. Arendt, *The Life of the Mind,* vol. 1, 20.

85. Arendt, *The Life of the Mind,* vol. 1, 21.

86. Arendt, *The Life of the Mind,* vol. 1, 27.

87. Arendt, *The Life of the Mind,* vol. 1, 27.

88. Arendt, *The Life of the Mind,* vol. 1, 27.

89. Arendt, *The Life of the Mind,* vol. 1, 28.

90. Clifford Geertz, *Local Knowledge* (New York: Basic Books, 1983), 3.

91. Paul Ricouer, "What Is a Text? Explanation and Understanding," in *Twentieth Century Literary Theory,* ed. Vassilis Lambropoulos and David Neal Miller (Albany, NY: SUNY Press, 1987), 337.

92. Stanley B. Messer, Louis A. Sass, and Robert L. Woolfolk, eds., *Hermeneutics and Psychological Theory* (New Brunswick, NJ: Rutgers University Press, 1988), 53.

93. Arendt, *Between Past and Future,* 157.

94. Arendt, *The Life of the Mind,* vol. 1, 21.

95. David Wood, ed., *On Paul Ricoeur: Narrative and Interpretation* (London: Routledge, 1991), 28.

96. David Carr, *Time: Narrative and History* (Bloomington: Indiana University Press, 1991), 4–5.

97. Carr, *Time,* 16.

98. Carr, *Time,* 65.

99. Carr, *Time,* 73.

100. Carr, *Time,* 18.

101. Carr, *Time,* 21.

102. Carr, *Time,* 22.

103. Carr, *Time,* 122.

104. Carr, *Time,* 122.

105. Carr, *Time,* 122.

106. Carr, *Time,* 129.

107. Carr, *Time,* 129.

108. Carr, *Time,* 147.

109. Carr, *Time,* 153.

110. Carr, *Time,* 153,

111. Arendt, *The Life of the Mind,* vol. 1, 180.

112. Arendt, *The Life of the Mind,* vol. 1, 21–22.

113. David Carr, "Reply to Ricouer," in David Wood, ed., *On Paul Ricouer,* 165–66.

114. Arendt, *The Human Condition,* 184.

115. Arendt, *The Origins of Totalitarianism,* xv.

3

The Problem of "The Political"

~ 1 ~

Conceptualizing what constitutes political activity is often considered to be the target of Arendt's work. As is the case with totalitarianism, her concept of *political activity* is also regarded as having a certain quirkiness about it. Parekh, for instance, stressing that Arendt sees "the universe . . . like a theater" where "[e]very living organism strives to appear and take part in the great 'play' of the world," describes her as "almost alone in the history of political philosophy to view politics as an aesthetic activity. . . . Arendt subsumes politics under *beauty*. For her it is primarily concerned to make the world beautiful. . . ."[1] This badly misstates the case, failing to see that for Arendt, politics is not *concerned* with anything at all; it is rather the definition of a livable world. We cannot immediately grasp this meaning of *political activity* in Arendt's work because it emerges at the end of a trail that takes us through the life of the mind beginning with the disclosure, by thinking toward the meaning of the self, of the experience of being freedom.

Arendt's work is a radical critique of the idea of freedom, the traditional concern for political theorizing. For Arendt, freedom is the expression of political activity, not the object of its concern. In this respect her work refuses "the blackmail of the Enlightenment" as Villa says, using a phrase coined by Michel Foucault.[2] Arendt expresses this by tracing the meaning of freedom in the history of the shifting relationships between two terms: the *vita activa* and the *vita contemplativa*.

"The term [vita activa] itself," Arendt points out, "in medieval philosophy [is] the standard translation of the Aristotelian *bios politikos:* . . . a life devoted to public-political matters." Aristotle's "*bios politikos*

79

denoted explicitly only the realm of human affairs"[3] that was the place where authentically free individuals must live their lives. It was in the life of the *polis* that individuals could live a truly human life of freedom beyond the command of necessity. Today, of course, we still conceive of freedom as a life liberated from necessity, but for the ancient Greeks this life had no other meaning than that of the *bios politikos*. Living the public life did not prove that they were free, as if freedom were an experience located beyond public view; living the public life was constitutive of the experience of freedom. Furthermore, it was living the public life that made the private life meaningful. "Man was taught by his polis," Weintraub tells us, "to perceive his very essence in being a *zoon politikon*, a polis creature, a public man. He had no freedom to choose between a life committed to the public good and a decent private life. The good private life was derived from the good life obtained as citizen only."[4] The ancient Greek, as Arendt pointedly tells us, experienced "freedom . . . as an 'outer manifestation,' not as an 'inner feeling.'"[5]

With the advent of Christianity the experience of freedom was relocated to what Bernauer calls "dedication to the self [that] grounds a constellation of Christian positions which debase the life of action and transform a potentially worldly agent into a pilgrim on earth, a *homo viator*."[6] Christianity, Arendt agrees, demeaned the life of political action, proclaiming a "freedom from politics, a freedom which is politically perhaps the most relevant part of our Christian heritage."[7] Christianity transformed "worldly experiences . . . into experiences within one's own self."[8] Freedom became the inner experience of a perfect spiritual peace, a perfection achieved by devaluing the noisy tumult of the vita activa. Life in the world contained no definition of freedom. Freedom was a truth beyond the world that was the road to an experience beyond understanding. As Arendt points out:

> Every movement of body and soul as well of speech and reasoning, must cease before truth. Truth, be it the ancient truth of Being or the Christian truth of the living God, can reveal itself only in complete human stillness. . . . Traditionally, therefore, the term *vita activa* receives its meaning from the *vita contemplativa;* its very restricted dignity is bestowed upon it because it serves the needs and wants of contemplation in a living body.[9]

Bernauer, quoting from Matthew 16:26, puts it this way: "The self is the temple of God and 'What profit would a man show if he were to gain the whole world and destroy himself in the process?'"[10] Arendt also points out that of course "the enormous superiority of contemplation over activity of any kind, action not excluded, is not Christian in origin. We find it in Plato's political philosophy, where the whole utopian reorganization of *polis* life is not only directed by the superior insight of the philosopher but has no aim other than to make possible the philosopher's way of life."[11]

With our modernity the world of ordinary life came into view. If for the ancient Greeks the world of ordinary life supported the meaningful life of political activity, and for medieval Christians it supported the worship of an invisible God, for men in the modern secular era the world became the arena for understanding the truth of ordinary life. As Kramer points out:

> Truth would be tied no longer to sacred writings and divine revelations, but would be seen henceforward as the product of close analysis and wide ranging debate. If the old order, with its pious sublimity and its monstrous vindictiveness, had received its highest expression in the work of Dante, the new order would be captured most gracefully in the tolerance, reasonableness and eloquence of John Stuart Mill. Earnestness, in short, would carry the day. . . . Mill maintained, with characteristic elegance, that most frequently "conflicting doctrines, instead of being one true and the other false, share the truth between them, and the nonconforming opinion is needed to supply the remainder of the truth of which the received doctrine embodies only a part." . . . Christianity's Via Dolorosa had been replaced by the earnest *via media* of the new age.[12]

Truth in the modern world is pursued by assembling fragmentary experiences refereed by dispassionate reason. The model for pursuing truth is work, and the model for the work of pursuing truth is scientific work. Truth is to be found by actively experiencing the world; truth that leaves the world behind is meaningless. On the surface, this looks like a reversal of the priority of the vita contemplativa over the vita activa. It only repeats, however, in different terms the framework within which the vita contemplativa came to be valued over the vita activa. If in medieval life, as Funkenstein has observed, "[t]he *vita contem-*

plativa . . . is not Everyman's talent . . . [h]ow different was the ethos of the Enlightenment! At the center of its self-understanding stood neither the 'revival of paganism' nor science for science's sake, but rather the duty of enlightening, of spreading the light of reason everywhere. The enlightener of the eighteenth century, contrary to his counterpart in the Middle Ages, believed therefore in the capacity of every person, high or low, to be educated, to acquire all knowledge."[13]

Under the banner of the Enlightenment every individual has the responsibility to become educated in the truth of who he is. In the modern world, discourse, debate, and speech in a public forum called *political* have value as they once did for the ancient Greeks, but not because they display freedom as a meaningful way of life. What they display is the project of making history. The world is still a road, as it once was for medieval Christians, which now however leads to our experience of freedom like a timeless eternal truth at the end of history. Utopian thought may now be political rather than Christian, but it is no less utopian. We still dream of inhabiting a peaceful world that will last forever. Political action is the engine of history, and as Arendt comments dryly, "[o]nly if seen in the image of working activity, could political action be trusted to produce lasting results."[14]

Arendt pursues the theme of "producing freedom" by distinguishing between *labor* and *work:*

> Labor is the activity which corresponds to the biological process of the human body, whose spontaneous growth, metabolism and eventual decay are bound to the vital necessities produced and fed into the life process by labor. The human condition of labor is life itself. Work is the activity which corresponds to the unnaturalness of human existence, which is not imbedded in, and whose mortality is not compensated by, the species ever recurring life cycle. Work provides an "artificial" world of things, distinctly different from all natural surroundings. Within its borders each individual life is housed, while this world itself is meant to outlast and transcend them all. The human condition of work is worldliness.[15]

We have come to experience ourselves pursuing freedom in the work of building an enduring world. Freedom for Arendt, however, is not experienced in the work of constructing and assembling a world designed and constructed by sociopolitical institutions. The modern world may have begun by restoring visibility to the world and political activity, but both fall under the image of a world working to progress in time toward what is contemplated as a unified world that promises the true experience of freedom.

Arendt sees the rearrangement of the priority of the vita activa over the vita contemplativa, heralded as the advent of modernity, as an illusion. Marxism, with its literalizing of the idea of human work fueling the dialectical movement of history as progress toward the end of history, is the obvious example of the illusion of this rearrangement. But only the *obvious* example. All of the formulas of modernity are echoes of the old formula of Plato as Arendt states it: "[T]he rise of the activity of the craftsman in the scale of estimations makes its first dramatic appearance in the Platonic dialogues. Labor, to be sure, remained at the bottom but political activity as something necessary for the life of contemplation was now recognized only to the extent that it could be pursued in the same way as the activity of the craftsman."[16] Political activity became an activity less real than the contemplated truth that commands it:

> Plato thought that human affairs, . . . the outcome of action, . . . should not be treated with great seriousness; the actions of men appear like the gestures of puppets led by an invisible hand behind the scene, so that man seems to be a kind of plaything of a god. It is noteworthy that Plato, who had no inkling of the modern concept of history, should have been the first to invent the metaphor of an actor behind the scenes who, behind the backs of acting men, pulls the strings and is responsible for the story.[17]

In the modern world the identity of everybody, politician or not, is like a commodity whose value is measured on a scale that penetrates into the space of the world, somewhat like Umberto Eco's metaphor for Foucault's pendulum, from an eternal, immobile, invisible point above and beyond the material world. What is measured is everybody's identity as a *thing* whose work *contributes* to ending the conflicts, tensions, disputes that the ancient Greeks once recognized as the display of freedom in the political life of the polis but is now identified with the noisy clamor of history transcending its own tensions toward a reign of peace identified with the inner experience of freedom.

Freedom, on the other hand, for Arendt is not something men work for, but display in "[a]ction, the only activity that goes on directly between men without the intermediary of things or matter, [which] corresponds to the human condition of plurality, to the fact that men, not Man, live on the earth and inhabit the world."[18] Freedom is not displayed in the material world men work to build, but in their activity of persuasion, argument, disputation that must take place in a pluralistic world where things seemingly fixed in commonsense meanings can nevertheless mean different things to different people. What Arendt is pointing to is something specific and concrete: The need to revitalize the idea of the vita activa put in disrepute when freedom became the standard of truth in the West by which to judge the life of every person. Great men are exemplary men—those judged having committed their lives to the true cause. Arendt, however, seeking to revitalize the vita activa, summons us to pay attention to those she calls the pre-Platonic Greeks[19] who were preoccupied with the question of how to judge the greatness of a man. They were those for whom *The Iliad* and *The Odyssey* were not history, myth, nor testament but, as Finley has pointed out, a living "vicarious experience"[20] that answered the question of which life was worth knowing and telling about because it was a "great life." Arendt summons us to consider a world in which "[t]he singer, servant of the Muses, sings 'the glorious deeds of men of old and the blessed gods,' but nowhere, as far as I can see, 'the glorious deeds of the gods,'[21] so that we can "think what we are doing."[22]

The pre-Platonic Greeks made a critical distinction between *behavior* and *action* that was lost after Plato, along with their meaning of freedom, that determined which life is worth knowing and telling about. The pre-Platonic Greeks were fully aware that as living human beings they *behaved,* and their behavior had consequences. As Arendt describes it, they judged "human behavior . . . like all civilized people . . . according to 'moral standards,' taking into account motives and intentions on the one hand and aims and consequences on the other. . . . "[23] In sum, the pre-Platonic Greeks judged behavior in terms of a set of universal external standards that included moral principles. The necessity of social order placed everybody under the command to live a right life that always involved then, as it does now, a degree of surrender of personal autonomy to the community. Living a right life, however, had nothing to do with being judged a great man. A great man was someone who performed a great action, and "action can be judged only by the criterion of greatness because it is in its nature to break through the commonly accepted and reach into the extraordinary, where whatever is true in common and everyday life no longer applies because everything that exists is unique and *suis generis.*"[24]

For the pre-Platonic Greeks, great acts were not those that are commanded by the need for social order. Social order was necessary because its absence could result in catastrophe. This, however, simply meant that social order was a natural state of affairs found, in one form or another, among all living things. Great acts were those that displayed the actor as someone who transcended the commands of nature to which all behaving creatures must submit, and who therefore was worthy of being immortalized by a story. A right life was not a life worth telling because it would tell *what* someone is rather than *who* he is. In fact, stories could not be told about those whose lives were part of the endless cycle of nature obedient to the law that commands all living things to eventually die because stories were worthy of being told only about human individuals and not mere living things.

For the pre-Platonic Greeks, knowing that everything humans say, do, and build perishes defined the paradox at the heart of their existence. "This paradox," Arendt points out, "that greatness was understood in terms of permanence while human greatness was seen in precisely the most futile and least lasting activities of men, has haunted Greek poetry and historiography as it has perturbed the quiet of philosophers."[25] The Greeks who suffered this paradox turned to the idea of *great acts* to affirm that as human beings they were more than creatures who could only behave, living right lives under the command of necessity as were their slaves.

"The early Greek solution to the paradox," Arendt tells us, "was poetic and non-philosophical. It consisted in the immortal fame which the poets could bestow upon word and deed to make them outlast not only the futile moment of speech and action but even the mortal life of their agent."[26] Listening to stories that would enshrine forever the great acts of individual mortal heroes, the pre-Platonic Greeks knew that they themselves were beings who possessed freedom from the commands of nature, unlike animals and slaves who could only behave. "The human capacity to achieve [immortality] was remembrance, Mnemosyne, who therefore was regarded as the mother of all other muses."[27]

The extraordinary nature of an act made it memorable. Motivation helped understand the extraordinary act of course, but action was extraordinary because its motivation was free of serving some cause such as the orderliness and preservation of the community. An act was extraordinary because the only cause it served was the honor of the actor. The rage of Achilles, which opens the *Iliad* and that carries the poem to its conclusion, was provoked by what Finley points out was Achilles's refusal of Agamemnon's "proper, and under all normal circumstances satisfactory, gift of amends . . ."[28] for refusing to give up the slave girl coveted by Achilles. Achilles, equal in status to Agamemnon and superior in fighting prowess, can be said to have been in a rage against the necessity of all mortals to have a position in the world—an identity—that is subject to changes in time and circumstance that expose them to experiencing the dishonor of abjection. Achilles's solution was to redeem his abjection by great acts that opposed the need for identity demanded of mortal humans.

Arendt states it this way: "[W]hoever consciously aims at being 'essential' [i.e., stripped of whatever is ephemeral] leaving behind a story and an identity which will win 'immortal fame,' must not only risk his life but expressly choose, as Achilles did, a short life and premature death. Only a man who does not survive his one supreme act remains the indisputable master of his identity and possible greatness, because he withdraws into death from the possible consequences and continuation of what he began."[29] Achilles had been taught by the gods to be "both a speaker of words and a doer of deeds," but neither his words nor his acts were to bring him immortality because they served some cause. Martyrdom was alien to the Homeric heroes, as Finley describes them:

> The Homeric heroes loved life fiercely, as they did and felt everything with passion, and no less martyr-like characters could be imagined; but even life must surrender to honour. The two central figures of the *Iliad,* Achilles and Hector, were both fated to live short lives, and both knew it. They were heroes not because at the call of duty they marched proudly to their deaths, singing hymns to God and country—on the contrary, they railed openly against their doom, and Achilles, at least, did not complain less after he reached Hades—but because at the call of honour they obeyed the code of the hero without flinching and without questioning.[30]

The judgment that a life was worth telling was made on the basis of an act deemed to be great because it transcended all compulsions, displaying the immortality of the free actor. Great action, Finley points out, was always action performed by a particular individual: "[T]he honour of the hero was purely individual, something he lived for and fought for only for its sake and for his own sake. . . . The honour of a community was a totally different quality, requiring another order of skills and virtues: in fact, the community could grow only by taming the hero and blunting the free exercise of his prowess, and a domesticated hero was a contradiction in terms."[31] As was, of course, an advanced, stable polis populated by Homeric heroes.

Gouldner, in his study of the sociological impact of Plato's influence, describes the taming of the hero during the evolution of the polis in these terms: "When complex forms of community organization developed with the later emergence of the *polis,* the requirements for the maintenance of the new urban social order and the old Homeric military values were dissonant, and the two can hardly be said to have ever attained a stable mutual accommodation."[32] The traits of the warrior did not become anachronistic, but were put to use when called for in the service of the community. "The 'quiet' virtues," Gouldner tells us, "as Adkins terms them, stressing cooperativeness or making cooperation feasible—such as temperance, civic service, justice and wisdom—in time became more salient."[33] For Arendt, it is momentous that those "salient" virtues were enshrined as eternal truths, signifying that the passing of the pre-Platonic Greeks was accompanied by prioritizing the vita contemplativa over the vita activa.[34]

What is at stake in Arendt's revitalizing the idea of the vita activa is not restoring the idea of the *hero,* but the idea that heroic actions represent individuating actions. What is at stake for her is restoring the idea of each human as an individual who accomplishes "great deeds" and "speaks great words" when he displays his freedom. In the cosmology of the pre-Platonic Greeks extraordinary actions display freedom as freedom from identity, the necessary condition for mortal humans to act. For Arendt, however, identity—the burden that humans must bear, imposed by the paradoxical experience of the meaning of the self to itself first described by Kierkegaard—is what freedom displays, not transcends, through human action. Drawing our attention to the pre-Platonic Greeks, Arendt is not seeking to restore the priority of the vita activa over the vita contemplativa. She is seeking to restore our way of understanding individuating action that was lost to modernity with the loss of the Homeric notion of a *great act* that cannot be described in terms of some abstract, universal principle of action, but only in terms of the concrete experiences of a particular individual of his freedom. Restoring the idea that action displays individual freedom constitutes a challenge to Arendt to conceptualize a new relationship between the ancient categories of vita activa and vita contemplativa in terms of a relationship between thinking and acting. It is necessary to consider this new relationship in order to grasp what Arendt means by political activity, no longer defined as a special class of acts mandated to fabricate a peaceful world that will rise above the tumult and uncertainties of individuals acting in a pluralistic world.

The new relationship Arendt posits between thinking and acting rests on the foundation of a radical idea: If action is always located in the world, the world is precisely where we are not when we think. The answer to the seemingly strange question *"Where are we when we think?"* that is the title of the last part of the first volume of her *The Life of the Mind* points to Arendt's concept of political action. And her point of departure for answering the question is a parable by one of the least political of men: Franz Kafka.

~ 2 ~

The awesome distinctiveness of Kafka's works increases when we read those who write about reading him. Kafka's depictions of what is going on and being said are always precise, exact, and never obscure, but as Thorlby points out, "the context is mysterious beyond all comprehension, and quite inconceivable as an imitation of life."[35] Kafka's work demands interpretation, and this mode of reading him spans a spectrum anchored on one end by interpretations of his work as the sublimation of an Oedipal relationship to his father, and on the other end as a linguistic demonstration of the impossibility of interpreting the true meaning of anything. In between, the spectrum runs through linking his work to Jewish tradition or to diagnosing the inhuman forces that rule the twentieth century.

Arendt's own reading of Kafka accepts him as a diagnostician of the baleful social structures of our time, but more importantly of the human condition in general. Arendt does not read Kafka as a prophet of doom, but a visionary who "wanted to build up a world in accordance with human needs and human dignities, a world where man's actions are determined by himself, and which is ruled by his laws and not by mysterious forces emanating from above or from below."[36] For Arendt, central to Kafka's diagnoses is one of his short parables that she reprints from the collection entitled *HE*. In this parable, "He" is battling two antagonists, one of whom attacks him from behind, and the other from the front. What He dreams of is that in the dark of some night he can jump out of the fight into the position of an umpire who will oversee the fight between his two antagonists.[37]

Arendt interprets Kafka's parable as analyzing poetically our "'inner state' in regard to time, of which we are aware when we . . . find our mental activities recoiling characteristically upon themselves. . . ."[38] The parable does not apply "to man in his everyday occupations but only to the thinking ego, to the extent that it has withdrawn from the business of everyday life. The gap between past and future opens only in reflection. . . ."[39] In other words, Kafka's parable depicts the moment in our experience of withdrawing from the world in preparation for thinking before we have actually begun to think. In this respect the battle that He is embroiled in is not going on in the world. He's struggle is taking place at the point called the *now*, at which the past and future meet. The now, however, is not a place in the world with objectively defined boundaries. It is a subjective space that in a real sense is not a place in the world at all but is He himself lifted out of the story he lives in—the world by which he struggles to understand, and make others understand, who he is. The *now* that He experiences is defined by expectations of future actions not yet performed based on his memory of past actions that no longer exist.

Arendt is making two critical points about the parable: First, it is the insertion of man into the world that accounts for the linear movement of time from past to future through the present:

[T]he time continuum, everlasting change, is broken up into the tenses past, present, future, whereby past and future are antagonistic to each other as the no-longer and the not-yet only because of the presence of man, who himself has an "origin," his birth, and an end, his death, and therefore stands at any given moment between them; this in-between is called the present. . . . It is the insertion of man with his limited life span

that transforms the continuously flowing stream of sheer change—
which we can conceive of cyclically as well as in the form of rectilin-
ear motion without ever being able to conceive of an absolute beginning
or an absolute end—into time as we know it.[40]

Put in other terms, Arendt reads the parable as translating the condition for the self thinking toward the meaning of itself—its paradoxical
experience of itself—into the metaphor of a temporal battleground. In
order to pursue the question of the meaning of himself, He must confront his past as a story that began before he began but whose beginning
nobody knows. It is only on the foundation of a story with a veiled origin and a veiled future that any self can think about the meaning of
itself. "[S]tories," as Arendt puts it, "the results of actions and speech,
reveal an agent, but this agent is not an author or producer."[41] The self's
ineradicable paradoxical experience of being a specific, unique individual before it knows the meaning of itself becomes, in Kafka's parable, a battleground over the coherency of the self's appearance to itself.
This is the terrible vulnerability with which He struggles.

It is over the issue of He's response to his struggle for coherency that
Arendt makes her second point about Kafka's parable. Although we are
not told He's intentions, they can be construed from his dream that in
the darkest of all nights he can achieve victory over the battling forces
only by jumping out of the fighting to become the "umpire over his
antagonists." What kind of umpire does He dream of becoming? Surely,
someone with the authority to straighten things out when they become
incoherent, to keep things going by arbitration that settles conflicts. If
what must be kept going is the forward motion of existence itself, what
are the rules for that forward movement of existence that gives the
umpire his authority to arbitrate? Kafka's parable implies that these
rules are contained in what He needs to experience himself as a coherent identity in the world: the capability of telling a story when asked
Who are you? and *What is going on here?* in which there would be perfect continuity between his remembered past and expected future
actions. Without this capability, He is subject to the horrendous experience of being transposed from the agent of his actions to a plaything of
every chance event encountered in the world. He is vulnerable to the
experience of chaotic incoherence, the description of which Kafka is an
acknowledged master.

Kafka's parable, however, also implies that as long as He seeks coherency in terms of a story with an unbroken continuity between past and future, he will never stop being embroiled in an endless struggle between them. The future holds no guarantee of a coherently continuous story because its outcome fades into the dark unknown of the network of relationships with others, while the story of his past reveals that he has never been the author or producer of the story about himself that he has already lived. He wants the impossible: to possess himself by erasing the gap between *who* and *what* he is that is opened by acting in a scene in which he has been and must always be simultaneously the spectator and the spectacle, appearing to himself as the unique agent of unique actions in a unique story, while appearing to others as "a type or a 'character'"[42] (to use Arendt's phrase) in someone else's story. He dreams of appearing coherent to himself by possessing himself not unlike a Homeric hero leaping out of his identity in the world because, like a leaky stopcock, his worldly identity drains his experience of being a unique agent of unique actions into a story that displays him as a *what* rather than a *who*.

In other parallel terms, He dreams of finding what Kafka once called an "Archimedean point"[43] above the world from which, no longer subject to the vicissitudes of time, He could straighten out the conflict between his past and future. Once that were straightened out, He would have the certainty of a continuous identity in a story that would always be about him from beginning to end as if he were its author and producer, no matter what he does or what is done to him. He would epitomize the autonomous self grounded like an immovable rock on the certainty of who he is in the midst of life's vicissitudes.

Arendt does not regard He's dream as bizarre. His dream is in effect the dream of valuing the vita contemplativa over the vita activa that has animated the history of the Western world for centuries. As Arendt puts it:

What are this dream and this region but the old dream Western metaphysics has dreamt from Parmenides to Hegel, of a timeless region, an eternal presence in complete quiet, lying beyond human clocks and calendars altogether, the region precisely, of thought? And what is the "position of umpire," the desire for which prompts the dream, but the seat of Pythagoras' spectators, who are the "best" because they do not participate in the struggle for fame and gain, are disinterested, uncommitted, undisturbed, intent only on the spectacle itself? It is they who can find out its meaning and judge the performance.[44]

As Arendt sees it, it was Descartes who set this dream into motion by moving "the Archimedean point into man himself to choose as ultimate point of reference the pattern of the human mind itself, which assures itself of reality and certainty within a framework of mathematical formulas which are its own products."[45] What else does Kafka's Archimedean point reflect but the scientific viewpoint, which originated, whether with Descartes or not, with the conviction that there is a coherent relationship between all events and happenings in the world because they are, in Arendt's words, "considered to be subject to a universally valid law in the fullest sense of the word, which means among other things, valid beyond the reach of human sense experience (even of the sense experiences made with the help of the finest instruments), valid beyond the reach of human memory and the appearance of mankind on earth, valid even beyond the coming into existence of organic life and the earth itself."[46]

Finding the Archimedean point is assuming that the lawful authority of the umpire will resolve the battles between past and future that rage in every individual so that they can know the unfolding story of their lives as coherently continuous stories from beginning to end at a single glance. Kafka, of course, is a supreme ironist who knows only too well, as he says in his parable about the Archimedean point, that "[h]e found the Archimedean point, but he used it against himself; it seems that he was permitted to find it only under this condition."[47] To dream that we can become coherent to ourselves, in other words, is to invoke eternal laws that place the experience of existing under the rule of abstract "processes"—a concept that allows us to think about our life only as a continuous flow of events and actions from beginning to end. The dream of discovering the Archimedean point is a dream of discovering a fulcrum from which to apply the leverage that shapes the movement of human lives.

But who applies the leverage? Process has no face; we can only imagine it with a beginning and an end, but we cannot imagine it as having a corporeal existence. We find ourselves at the receiving end of the lever wielded, to use Arendt's term, by the "nobody"[48] we ourselves have created. We have created, in brief, a Kafkaesque world where we feel the palpable pressure of being ruled by an anonymous maze of economic, psychological, sociological, and political processes that command obedience in the name of eternal laws governing all living things.

If we juxtapose Kafka's ironic parable about the discovery of the Archimedean point to his parable about He, it is possible to say that Arendt reads Kafka as unable to find his way toward a human world in which everyone would determine their own actions. Kafka's failing his own vision is what prompts Arendt to revise his parable about He. Before turning to her revision however, it is worth considering an interpretation by Christopher Goodden of Kafka's story, "The Great Wall of China."[49] In terms of this story Goodden does not read Kafka as failing his vision, and the contrast with Arendt in this regard helps put her revision in sharp relief.

Kafka's story concerns the process of constructing the Great Wall of China ostensibly for protection against barbarian invasions from the North. Goodden argues compellingly that the story itself presents a number of plausible reasons why this cannot be construed to be the true purpose for the construction of the wall. Goodden interprets the "ulterior motive" for building the wall to be that of a "quest," which he defines as the pursuit of "a *modus vivendi* which is psychologically and existentially comfortable . . . guaranteed by the selection of an impossible goal or the recognition of some unreal or implacable foe."[50] In the cool language of utilitarian reasoning Goodden elaborates on what he means by a "comfortable" modus vivendi: One in which "the psychological and existential benefits of building the wall outweigh the benefits of not building it." The wall, in fact, "was started as the preferable alternative to an extra-quest predicament."[51] We do not find this language, however, cast in cost–benefit terms matching Kafka's own language. Kafka describes the predicament that the quest for a wall seeks to solve as no less than the terrifying force of human nature: "Human nature, essentially changeable, unstable as the dust, can endure no restraint; if it binds itself it soon begins to tear madly at its bonds, until it rends everything asunder, the wall, the bonds, and its very self."[52]

The construction of the Great Wall is an endless process because the builders are building against themselves and the stakes of the game are the highest. Kafka clearly implies that the nature of every human being is such that, uncontained by a structure of continuity, it can create a catastrophe that destroys identity itself. Goodden cites the river analogy Kafka uses in the story to that effect: "[T]he builders of the wall are strengthening the river banks of their existence, so that on the one hand they do not spill out and on the other (and conversely) so that they maintain the original shape, formation and direction of their existence. . . . [T]he wall is a kind of defining agent. It draws attention to the identity of the subject."[53] This interpretation reveals that the "subject can be seen to be in league with his enemy."[54] It is a Hegelian conclusion: identity requires a struggle with another who opposes it.

Goodden reads the struggle between human nature and identity in Kafka's story to be part of an evolving process in which the endless repetitive labor of constructing a great wall is persistently accompanied by a crisis of consciousness that always carries mankind to the brink of catastrophe from which they then pull back. Although men are persistently carried to the brink they do not step over, which is why Goodden does not read Kafka as a prophet of doom. Goodden's reading relies on the process of consciousness evolving, by virtue of its crisis, to a point where it will ultimately "annihilate all traces of the quest and its intellectual dishonesty, leaving the critical mind free to readjust itself to its new-found freedom."[55]

In these terms Goodden creates an ending to Kafka's story that Kafka did not write but is correlative with the modern idea of "discovering freedom." Freedom is like a long-lost treasure that we seek like explorers in a wilderness who know neither where they are nor the exact nature of the treasure they are looking for. And as is the usual case in such stories, the moment of discovery, when and if it comes, will catch us from behind when the process of exploration that impels us forward suddenly pushes us to where the treasure is in sight.

In a sense, such stories hold us in thrall because the activity of exploration is very much like waiting for something to appear, as if in a dream. While it is undeniable that Kafka's work in general shows us that living under the rule of nobody is accompanied by a persistent crisis of consciousness, in "The Great Wall of China," however, he depicts the crisis in terms of an ironic, self-defeating futility of waiting for an anonymous process to liberate us from being servile to an anonymous process. This is depicted in a parable told by an anonymous narrator to someone anonymous who is waiting somewhere in China for a message sent to him alone from the dying Emperor. The Emperor's messenger, however, finds it impossible to push his way through the crowds in the palace: even

> [I]f at last he should burst through the outermost gate—but never, never can that happen—the imperial capital would lie before him, the center of the world, crammed to bursting with its own sediment. Nobody could fight his way through here even with a message from a dead man. But you sit at your window when the evening falls and dream it to yourself. Just so, as hopelessly and hopefully, do our people regard the Emperor. They do not know what Emperor is reigning, and there exist doubts regarding even the name of the dynasty.[56]

This parable within the story does not suggest that Kafka had Goodden's ending in mind, if indeed it is possible to say that Kafka had any ending in mind. The irony of calling on a process in order to be liberated from a process can only leave the caller sitting and dreaming forever at a window. While Arendt's revision of Kafka's parable about He can reasonably be said to supply it with an ending Kafka never wrote or even had in mind, her's is an ending that opposes men's propensity to wait for a process to carry them to a place where they dream of being free of faceless processes that rule them. Kafka's parable about He fails because it represents He, the *thinking ego,* as a dreamer and not as a thinker, and for Arendt dreaming is a far cry from thinking. The difference between them marks the need to radically redefine what it means for the self to experience a coherent meaning of itself. If, to use Goodden's terms, there are persistent and chronic crises of consciousness that carry us to the brink, then we can say that Arendt's redefinition of what it means for the self to be coherent to itself calls for it to step off the brink rather than draw back into a state of dreaming.

To think toward the meaning of ourselves is to step off the brink, because it is then that we "assume the position of 'umpire,' of arbiter and judge over the manifold, never-ending affairs of human existence in the world, never arriving at a final solution to their riddles but ready with ever-new answers to the question of what it may be all about."[57] This suggests that Arendt is retaining the metaphor of *umpire* for the figure of the *thinking ego* while radically revising its meaning. How shall we think of an umpire who is not arbitrating what he knows is going on, but is arbitrating a riddle by supplying new answers to what is going on? Such a notion of arbitration can settle nothing between the battling past and future. Indeed, it can only involve the umpire in the battle itself. As a thinking ego, He would still be in the role of umpire, observing the storm of events that define where he is *now* located in the world, but this now would be "the quiet in the center of a storm which, though totally unlike the storm, still belongs to it."[58] Put another way, Arendt wants to prevent us from defining thinking toward ourselves as playing the role of an umpire, which can settle anything.

Thinking not only settles nothing, it unsettles everything. It is true, of course, that when we think toward ourselves our past appears to us as a "historical fact." It is, however, the stories we tell about the facts that convey their meaning. When Arendt states that "who somebody essentially *is*, we know only after he is dead,"[59] she is telling us that it is only from a story's end that the past can gain a true meaning. This is not entirely so with respect to knowing who somebody "essentially is," since the history of every individual is a story within the larger story of the history of the group into which the individual was born that is a story without end. It would have been more accurate if Arendt had said that the *true* meaning of who somebody essentially is can never be known either by others after he is dead or by himself when, while alive, he is thinking toward the meaning of himself. But Arendt is quite right to stress that it is the *end* of a story that settles the meaning of everything that precedes it from its beginning. To use Miller's metaphor, a story is an endless "chase [that] has a beast in view. The end of the story is the retrospective revelation of the law of the whole. That law is an underlying 'truth' that ties all together in an inevitable sequence. . . ."[60]

To step back from the brink is to dream of leaving nothing unsettled; and this dream embraces the promise conveyed by the idea of *process* that is no more than a dream that the "beast" that we feel molesting the coherent meaning of our identity can and will be captured and killed. What else are stories about anonymous processes that determine the behavior of the world than promises sent to each individual who dreams of being part of a world in which he will find himself united with himself in the sense of being finally and safely in possession of himself? This kind of ending is crucial, because by defining the dream of self-possession we can settle the questions of who we are—have always been from the beginning—and what we must do and be to make our beginning lead to the right end. For an individual to dream of possessing himself he must assume that there is a truth to *who he is* before there is a story he can tell about himself, and that the story of the process to which his understanding of himself is subject gives him that truth formulated by the ending he dreams of. The story of the process that determines what he is calls him to be who he was always meant to be. The meaning of *who he is* is no longer a vexing riddle. The story of the process has lifted him above the turmoil that surrounds thinking about the question. It is now a matter of believing that he has only to meld his own individual story in a seamless unity with a story of a process, and wait for the process to fulfill its promise to carry him to whom he was always meant to be.

No one can escape the paradox that surrounds experiencing a coherent identity, which at least in Goodden's view drives them to the brink of a Kafkaesque crisis of consciousness. Stepping back from the brink, however, means individuals must sustain their belief that they are in the process of being transformed from something that has been corrupted and defiled into whom they were meant to be from the beginning. Relying on the promise of a process means there can be only one beginning and only one ending. Individuals must fix their eyes on the end, because it is the end that tells us there has been only one beginning that is privileged to be called *their* beginning because it is continuous with the end. Kafka knew that the dream of appearing coherent to oneself because one can tell a story about who one is that is continuous from beginning to end is a dream of destiny that not only works against the self, but also against every living thing.

What Arendt saw, that Kafka did not, is that the incorporation of the activity of thinking into his parable about He turns us away from the modern obsession with how stories must end—i.e., with *predictions, forecasts,* and *futurology,* the modern language of destiny. It is when we refuse the premise upon which the idea of *process* rests that allows us to experience only one beginning to the story we tell about ourselves that can lead to only one ending, we become capable of coherently experiencing ourselves as freedom that knows itself as freedom because its actions are capable of beginning something new.

We can now see Arendt's corrected image[61] of Kafka's embattled He in the full measure of its significance. In Kafka's parable the forces of the past and future meet head on, corresponding to the usual representation of the tenses that demarcate the movement of time as linked linearly. But Arendt insists that "thanks to the insertion of a fighting presence, they meet at an angle, and the correct image would then have to be what the physicists call a parallelogram of forces."[62] In the new image, "[i]deally, the action of the two forces that form our parallelogram should result in a third force, the resultant diagonal whose origin would be at the point at which the forces meet and upon which they act."[63] He, of course, is that meeting point, and Arendt labels the diagonal that results the "thought train": "This diagonal force, whose origin is known, whose direction is determined by past and future, but which exerts its force toward an undetermined end as though it could reach out into infinity, seems to me a perfect metaphor for the activity of thought."[64]

As a "thinking ego," Kafka could no longer describe He as an agonized dreamer dreaming of leaping above and beyond the world where he would be safe from its battling forces. For Arendt, a He that thinks toward the meaning of himself would be immersed in the quest for the meaning of his own embattled appearance of himself. Thinking begins by immersion in the world of appearances, and then withdrawal from the world in quest of the meaning of the appearance of one's own self as an unsolvable riddle. In other words, I am situated in the *now,* neither as an umpire who can resolve the battle between my past and my future nor as the allegorical character in Kafka's story, "The Great Wall of China," who dreams of a message sent just to me from a secret place where the Truth resides that will unite me with myself. I am the experience of the paradoxical identity—the unsolvable riddle—who, while knowing that I can never possess myself, also know that I possess the ability to act in a way that inserts something new into the story about myself. This "something new" to which the path of thinking leads is not simply the beginning of an event: it is, in a certain experiential sense, a new beginning of myself. Born once, I can never be born again, but now, at the end of the path of thinking, I am aware that I have never been certain that it was *I* who ever told my story because I was never certain that when I spoke, I was not speaking conventional thoughts—the thoughts of someone else or even an anonymous nobody.

I am now aware of the difference between hearing others speak with my voice and hearing myself speak. At the end of the path of thinking coherency adheres not to my identity that I can never possess, but to my act of speaking that makes humans capable of disrupting the inertia of the conventional with the extraordinary by beginning something new.

Arendt, bringing the Final Solution to bear on our own lives, seems to have put that which its perpetrators refused in the last sentences of *The Origins of Totalitarianism:* "Beginning, before it becomes a historical event, is the supreme capacity of man; politically it is identical with man's freedom. *Initium ut esset homo creatus est*—'that a beginning be made man was created' said Augustine. This beginning is guaranteed by each new birth; it is indeed every man."[65]

Arendt's revision of Kafka's parable about He supplies the answer to her own question, *Where are we when we think?* We are standing *now,* simultaneously in the world and withdrawn from it, carrying our origins to the brink of something new.

~ 3 ~

It is extremely rare to find people who have neutral feelings toward their natal origins rather than extremes of love or hate. Memory is essential to asserting a continuous identity, and this continuity depends on the ability to tell a continuous story about oneself. Intense feelings about one's natal origin, whether love or hate, are a measure of the degree to which a story that features them as a beginning supplies a stabilizing answer to the question, *Who am I?* Such a story is almost always experienced to be a product of reality and not the imagination because, as Mary Warnock observes, "though memory is often thought of in terms of images of the past, . . . it may most properly be thought of as a kind of knowledge, to which images are not essential, though they may be a frequent accompaniment."[66]

Stories in which individuals' natal origins are experienced as their only beginnings make meaningful the incontrovertible fact that individuals are all born "inserted," to use Arendt's oft-repeated term, into stories they never authored. *Insertion* becomes an incontrovertible beginning rather than a meaningless random event in a story in which individuals identify their birth, endowing them with a set of attributes and characteristics that are their *potentials* waiting to be actualized in their lives. It is this beginning that defines their struggle to possess themselves. From the point of view of stories that make sense of the experience of being inserted into someone else's story at birth, it does not matter whether individuals love or hate their natal origin. What matters is that the story identifies who they are as a struggle to possess themselves, and at the same time supplies a face to the molesters of the being they know they are meant to be with whom they are struggling.

The story of hating one's natal origin is the lot of the parvenu such as Rahel Varnhagen, who for a brief while in the eighteenth century held the best-known and most important salon in Berlin for artists and intellectuals. Arendt's rich and multifaceted study of her correspondence makes it clear that the potential that Varnhagen experienced and that made her into a special and superior person could be actualized only by identifying her natal origin as her nemesis:

> Thus Rahel wrote to David Veit, the friend of her youth: "I have a strange fancy: it is as if some supramundane being, just as I was thrust into this world, plunged these words like a dagger into my heart: Yes, have sensibility, see the world as few see it, be great and noble, nor can I take from you the faculty of eternally thinking. But I add one thing more: be a Jewess! And now my life is slow bleeding to death. . . . I can, if you will, derive every evil, every misfortune, every vexation from *that*."[67]

The more common story of loving one's natal origin is the story of an ethnic pride that so readily congeals into a story of a nation that, to quote Arendt, "represents the 'milieu' into which man was born, a closed society to which one belongs by right of birth."[68] To experience beginning as being born into a nation whose beginning preceded one's own is to identify with the emotionality surrounding what Brennan has termed "something more ancient and nebulous—the *nation*—a local community, a domicile, family, condition of belonging"[69] that must be defended against molestation.

Against such stories, Arendt argues precisely for a neutral feeling toward one's natal origin. She called her own natality no more than a "fact" in her response to Scholem, and even more contentiously, in a 1964 interview with the German journalist Günter Gaus, something she denied should be loved by anyone. Gaus asked Arendt: "As a politically active being, doesn't man need commitment to a group, a commitment that can then to a certain extent be called love? Are you not afraid that your attitude could be politically sterile?" Arendt answers:

No. I would say that it is the other attitude that is politically sterile. In the first place belonging to a group is a natural condition. You belong to some sort of group when you are born, always. But to belong to a group in the way that you mean, in a second sense, that is, to join or form an organized group, is something completely different. This kind of organization has to do with a relation to the world. People who become organized have in common what are ordinarily called interests. The directly personal relationship, where one can speak of love, exists of course, foremost in real love, and it also exists in a certain sense in friendship. There a person is addressed directly, independent of his relation to the world. . . . [I]f you confuse these things, if you bring love to the negotiating table, to put it bluntly, I find that fatal.[70]

We must be cautious not to extend the fatality Arendt sees in confusing one's interests with love for one's natal group to a condition in which it could be fatal not to identify one's interests with one's natal group. When one is attacked as a Jew, she once asserted in a different context, "[t]he only possibility [is] to fight back *as a Jew* and not as a human being . . . if you are attacked as a Jew, you cannot say 'Excuse me, I am not a Jew; I am a human being.' This is silly."[71] But it is not silly to fight for the purpose of being a human being who can transcend the presumed fatefulness of his natal origin.

Arendt's insistence on the importance of neutral feelings toward our natal origins contains two implied admonitions: not to be confused over what it means to *think,* and not to confuse our appearance in the world as our only beginning. Arendt's concept of thinking focuses us on both admonitions. *Thinking* is defined by Arendt as one of three faculties that constitutes the life of the mind. Her use of the metaphor *life of the mind* carries the risk of intimating that what is essential about being human beings is located in a space *inside* that demarcates them from the *outside* space of the world. Such a notion suggests that the mind contains the essence of human beings that is revealed by exploring its depth—an enterprise modeled by Freud, who troped himself as an archeologist excavating the mind.

Arendt's concept of the mind, however, does not refer us to a space where certain essential functions and mechanisms are located that can explain human behavior. The life of the mind, for Arendt, refers us to the activities of *thinking, willing,* and *judging* that can be described only by starting with, and never leaving behind, the experiencing subject whose primary experience is that of the appearance of things in the world, including himself: "Thinking, willing, and judging are the three basic mental activities; they cannot be derived from each other and though they have certain common characteristics they cannot be reduced to a common denominator."[72] Arendt insists on calling "these mental activities basic because they are autonomous; each of them obeys the laws inherent in the activity itself. . . ."[73]

We can say as well that they are basic because they correspond to basic experiences that, for want of a better term, we call *mental: thinking* corresponds to the experience of withdrawing from the world to contemplate events that are past, that no longer exist except in memory; *willing*, to the experience that nothing compels me to do the very project I have already willed myself to do; *judging*, to the experience that without knowing why, I know the difference between what is beautiful and ugly, good and bad, just and unjust, etc.

It is true, Arendt points out, that "[s]ince it is always the same person whose mind thinks, wills, and judges, the autonomous nature of these activities has created great difficulties." She elaborates on these difficulties:

> To be sure, the objects of my thinking or willing or judging, the mind's subject matter, are given in the world, or arise from my life in this world, but they themselves as activities are not necessitated or conditioned by either. Men . . . can mentally transcend all these conditions, but only mentally, never in reality. . . . They can judge affirmatively or negatively the realities they are born into and by which they are also conditioned; they can will the impossible, for instance eternal life; and they can think, that is speculate meaningfully, about the unknown and the unknowable. And although this can never directly change reality— indeed in our world there is no clearer or more radical opposition than that between thinking and doing—the principles by which we act and the criteria by which we conduct our lives depend ultimately on the life of the mind.[74]

The faculties of the mind do not function, alone or together, as an engine would function by impelling the subject to act. But does this mean that when we *do* act they are manifest in our actions? This is precisely what Arendt does *not* mean. The critical case-in-point is that of *thinking.* It is true that it appears that we are always thinking, in the sense of reflecting on matters we must deal with in everyday life. But for Arendt this is not thinking: "Consciousness, to be sure—Kant's 'I think'—not only accompanies 'all other representations' but all my activities. . . ." But Arendt points out that these are activities "in which nevertheless I can be oblivious of my self. Consciousness as such, before it is actualized in solitude, achieves nothing more than an awareness of the sameness of the I-am . . . which guarantees the identical continuity of a self throughout the manifold representations, experiences, and memories of a lifetime."[75]

In effect, *thinking,* identified with the activities of the self engaging the world, is not *thinking* as Arendt means it. We are thinking when we withdraw from the world into a soundless dialogue with ourselves whose subject is the representations of memory, and whose purpose is a quest for the meaning of what no longer exists: the appearance of the self in the manifold scenes of its life.

Thinking, in these terms, is a dismantling of the meaning of the self, modeled for Arendt, by the "pure" thinking of Socrates who claimed, to his ultimate misfortune, "the right to go about examining the opinions of other people, thinking about them and asking his interlocutors to do the same."[76] It is striking, Arendt observes, that "Plato's Socratic dialogues . . . are all aporetic. The argument either leads nowhere or goes around in circles. . . . None of the *logoi,* the arguments, ever stays put; they move around." The meaning of the words, ideas, or concepts with which they are concerned never seem to settle anywhere: "[W]hen we try to define them, they get slippery; when we talk about their meaning, nothing stays put anymore, everything begins to move."[77] As a result, "this kind of pondering reflection does not produce definitions and in that sense is entirely without results."[78]

The significance of using Socrates as the example of what it means to think toward the meaning of the self is to underscore that:

[T]hinking inevitably has a destructive, undermining effect on all established criteria, values, measurements of good and evil, in short, on those customs and rules of conduct we treat of in morals and ethics. These frozen thoughts, Socrates seems to say, come so handily that you can use them in your sleep; but if the wind of thinking, which I shall now stir in you, has shaken you from your sleep and made you fully awake and alive, then you will see that you have nothing in your grasp but perplexities, and the best we can do with them is share them with each other.[79]

Arendt, by calling us to become fully awake and alive by thinking toward the meaning of ourselves, must face the question that Socrates, her exemplary thinker, poses: If it is inescapable that thinking means surrendering the coherency of the thinking self's experience of itself; and if, as Kafka's work exemplifies, the coherency of that experience is the foundation for the possibility of humans acting in the world, then how can we escape, using Arendt's own words, "the reproach" that thinking is "impractical and useless" and "does not work?"[80] Put in other terms, how can Arendt imagine that she has a workable concept of thinking when she defines it as having a "destructive and under-mining effect" on everything that we depend on to stabilize the meaning of ourselves?

J. Glenn Gray states clearly what Arendt confronts in this reproach: "What troubles me most in [Arendt's] insistence on the reality of the contingent is its threat of meaninglessness."[81] What Arendt's concept of thinking threatens is the viability of the very idea of human freedom that she states categorically manifests itself in the activity of willing: "The decision the will arrives at can never be derived from the mechanics of desire or the deliberations of the intellect that may precede it. The will is either an organ of free spontaneity that interrupts all causal chains of motivation that would bind it or it is nothing but an illusion."[82] Gray summarizes Arendt's position this way:

> The hallmark of willing is our power to initiate something altogether new, something that we realize every instant we can also leave undone. Our will is the originator of actions that are not explicable by preceding causes. Such actions spring from the incalculable power of willing and are as spontaneous and unpredictable as life itself, which the will close-ly resembles. In contrast to reason, the will is our organ for the future; it possesses the power to make present to the mind the not-yet dimension of reality.[83]

Gray reproaches Arendt for not going beyond *willing* as the expression of freedom. She does not attempt to discover "the ground or ulti-mate source of our individual freedom"[84] so that we can avoid the feeling of freedom becoming "a doom in the Sartrean sense, a burden and a curse."[85] Gray correctly sees that in Arendt's view it would indeed be bizarre to declare the experience that "what I have decided to do I can leave undone" nothing but an illusion. At the same time, he views an experience of freedom that is not grounded outside the self's experience to be a despairing freedom. To couch *freedom,* as Gray does however, in the language of *accomplishment, goal, achievement,* or *task* is to risk displacing freedom from the act of willing as the possibility of always beginning something new. It also risks misunderstanding thinking by identifying it with reasoning the principles that must govern the will if it is to act to achieve freedom.

But for Arendt, while it is a contradiction in terms to say that thinking causes freedom to manifest itself in acts of willing, it is also impossible to say that thinking is therefore unrelated to willing. Thinking, "the power of representation," Arendt states, although "unable to move the will or provide judgment with general rules, must prepare the particulars given to the senses in such a way that the mind is able to handle them in their absence; it must, in brief, *de-sense* them."[86]

This preparation is her response to the reproach against thinking. If *thinking* removes us from the sensate world in quest of the meaning of what was and is no more, *willing* returns us to the sensate world, prepared by thinking to constitute the meaning of what appears in light of moving toward the future. What Arendt is underscoring is that the will is no less a faculty of mind that constitutes the meaning of the world than thinking is a faculty that constitutes the meaning of the past; by the same token, willing suffers from the inherent indeterminacy of meaning no less than does thinking. When we deal with thinking, the quest for the meaning of what was, as preparation for willing as action toward a future that is not yet, "we are dealing with matters that never were, that are not yet, and that may well never be."[87]

Thinking, which Arendt calls "a technique of dismantling,"[88] prepares willing by dismantling the meaning of the past as a story governed by reasoned principles of right action. What is left after the dismantling, Arendt tells us, "is still the past, but a *fragmented* past, which has lost its certainty of evaluation."[89] It is not clear, however, what Arendt means by the fragments of the past. Her own explication offers the lines from Shakespeare's *The Tempest* that begin "Full fathom five thy father lies," alluding to the "sea change" that turns his remains "into something rich and strange," as her way of saying it "better and more clearly than I could."[90]

Arendt's use of Shakespeare's lines is consistent with her attempts to define traditionally elusive ideas like *thinking* with the aid of rich metaphors. "I think that this 'thinking,'" she once wrote in a delivered paper—"thinking in the Socratic sense—is a maieutic function, a midwifery. That is, you bring out all your opinions, prejudices, what have you; and you know that never, in any of the [Platonic] dialogues did Socrates ever discover any child [of the mind] who was not a windegg." But then she goes on to say in the very next sentence, "[Y]ou remain in a way empty after thinking. . . ."[91] She is talking about this "emptiness" as a preparation for *judging,* and while it may be an appropriate metaphor in that context, it does not help us very much to understand the fragmenting of the past as thinking's preparation for *willing.*

In that context, I suggest that at least one thing Arendt is pointing to when she talks about thinking leaving behind fragments of the past rather than emptiness is that thinking leaves the thinking subject in a state of doubt rather than despair. The difference is significant. *Dismantling* the past does not mean opening a bottomless abyss into which I must plunge when I think. Arendt never tells me that thinking toward the meaning of myself releases me from the experience of being continuous with my past. Just the opposite. Without a past with which I can experience a continuity I can indeed, as a thinking ego, fall into an abyss from which I cannot return to the world as a being who can will his actions. The past that has a fixed grip on me cannot be abolished as a reality without abolishing the experience that I am real to myself. When I seek the meaning of myself in the memories of my past, I cannot treat my memories as if they were no more than images that I can erase after thinking about them, like those images produced by my imagination. To do so would be to become the incarnation of what Arendt has called the "frightening . . . notion of solipsistic freedom—the 'feeling' that my standing apart, isolated from everyone else, is due to free will, that nothing and nobody can be held responsible for it but me myself."[92]

Arendt might well have added that such a "feeling" is but a short step from feeling like a god who can give birth to itself at will. This danger, Sartre tells us in his inimitable way, is not a danger to which we are normally exposed: "No doubt recollection is, in many respects, very close to the image . . ." but there is an "essential difference" between them. A memory "is always real but *past.* It exists *past* which is one mode of real existence among others. And when I want to apprehend it anew, I pursue it *where it is.* . . . When I recall this or that memory I do not *call it forth* but I betake myself to where it is, I direct my consciousness to the past where it awaits me as real event in retirement."[93]

Arendt's notion of dismantling the past can be said to be the equivalent of the thinking subject carrying doubt to his past in his quest for its meaning. Doubt about the past becomes self-doubt, which in turn functions as the instrument for self-discovery. What is continuous in the sequence of *nows* that the thinking subject has already lived is not the progressive struggle to actualize the potential of his identity that was given to him with his beginning, but the struggle with the riddle or paradox about who he is that he cannot solve. The space of the now in which he stands as a thinking subject is no longer like a bridge that welds the past to the future in one continuous story about his life that could have had only one beginning. In the midst of the dismantled fragments of the meaning of his past he discovers himself as a radically individuated will prepared to "fashion," to use Arendt's word, those fragments "into an 'enduring I' that directs all particular acts of volition." It is this "fashioning" will that "creates the self's *character* and therefore was sometimes understood as the *principium individuationis,* the source of the person's specific identity."[94]

The will, assembling the fragments of the past into the *I* that appears to the self and is displayed to others, is the power to bring something new to the subject's story of his life, who understands himself as the continuous struggle, without beginning or end in sight, to make sense of his identity. This is a radically individuating discovery: The *new* is each individual's own *new,* framed, identified, and recognized by its departure from his own past, and not the past defined by a transcendental story with a universal beginning and end about everybody's life. In this sense, doubt has penetrated into the heart of the belief in progress, which has never faded as a guiding belief in the lives of those inheritors of Western tradition. The Other, always integral to the subject's understanding of who he is, is also integral to the contingency of his understanding: "The individual, fashioned by the will and aware that it could be different from what it is (character, unlike bodily appearance or talents and abilities, is not given to the self at birth) always tends to assert an 'I-myself' against an indefinite 'they'—all the others that I, as an individual, am *not*."⁹⁵

The significant discovery that the condition of freedom is founded on doubt is accompanied by an equally significant discovery: If thinking that carries self-doubt to the meaning of who I am by dismantling the meaning of my past prepares me to return to the world as a radically individuated will with the power to begin something new, then willing prepares me to discover the Other—not simply as a nemesis to possessing myself as the author of my life, but as an Other who is intelligible to me as the source of the doubt upon which my freedom is founded. In other words, *willing* prepares me for *judging*.

∿ **4** ∿

With the analysis of *judging* we have reached Arendt's unique definition of *The Political* that for us is the focal point for understanding the bearing that the Final Solution has on our time. Ironically, Arendt died before she could complete *The Life of the Mind*, containing her analysis of judging. She left behind, however, a number of sources from which it proved possible to reasonably construct what she would have said that would have completed her nullifying, in her terms, the feeling "that we are *doomed* to be free by virtue of being born. . . . This impasse, if such it is, cannot be opened or solved except by an appeal to another mental faculty, no less mysterious than the faculty of beginning, the faculty of Judgment. . . ."⁹⁶

For her analysis of judging, Arendt makes the startling appeal for inspiration to Kant's *Critique of Aesthetic Judgment,* because it offers "an analytic of the beautiful primarily from the viewpoint of the judging spectator."⁹⁷ What is important to her in this respect, Beiner points out, "is not Kant's aesthetic but his political sense. It is because of his awareness of the public quality of beauty and the public relevance of beautiful things, she maintains, that Kant insisted that judgments of taste are open to discussion and subject to dispute."⁹⁸ What is equally important is that Kant is consistent with Arendt in conceptualizing the judging not as a derivative of logical reasoning, but as the activity of an independent faculty of the mind that is directed specifically toward constituting the meaning of what appears in the world. Beiner puts it this way:

In aesthetic no less than in political judgments, a decision is made, and although this decision is always determined by a certain subjectivity, by the simple fact that each person occupies a place of his own from which he looks upon and judges the world, it also derives from the fact that the world itself is an objective datum, something common to all its inhabitants. The activity of taste decides how this world . . . is to look and sound, what men will see, and what they will hear in it.[99]

Arendt does not mean to identify judgments of taste with political judgments. She links them in order to break the link between what Beiner terms "judgment and philosophical argument oriented toward truth. The latter, demonstrable truth, seeks to *compel* agreement by a process of compelling proof. Judgments of taste, by contrast, are, like political opinions, persuasive; they are characterized by," and here he quotes Arendt, "'the hope of *coming* to an agreement with everyone else eventually.'"[100] In other words, we recognize philosophical arguments grounded in logical reasoning because they move from the general universal to the particular concrete, while judgments, whether aesthetic or political, can be recognized because they move in the reverse direction. "[W]e can and *do* make particular judgments all the time," Jackson points out, "whether we know what courage is, what beauty is, what justice is, or what evil is."[101]

The movement from the concrete particular to the general universal is the commonplace of making judgments, however embarrassing it may be to logical reasoning. There are multiple examples that can be culled from judgments of taste: who, while unable to state a universally valid definition of beauty, cannot say they know it when they see it? Arendt's favorite example, however, is one that is closer to political judgments: The jury that must deliberate justice when no one has ever been able to supply a universally valid definition for it. A jury is aware that all questions "are somehow *really* debatable" and "also aware that there are *different viewpoints,* from the two sides of the court trial, from which you could look at the issue."[102] Juries do not exist because it is possible to administer something defined as justice; they exist because the idea of justice exists on the foundation of doubting how to define it. Beiner clearly summarizes the general point Arendt is making from the example of juries, returning us to what thinking empties us of in the context of preparing us for judging:

According to Arendt, thought—the critical movement of thinking—loosens the hold of universals (e.g., entrenched moral habits ossified into inflexible general precepts) and thus frees judgment to operate in an open space of moral or aesthetic discrimination and discernment. Judgment functions best when this space has been cleared for it by critical thinking. In this way, the universal does not domineer over the particular; rather the latter can be apprehended as it truly discloses itself. . . . [T]hinking releases the political potency of the faculty of judgment—the potency that inheres in its capacity to perceive things as they are, that is, as they are phenomenally manifest.[103]

Judgment, in effect, joins *thinking* and *willing* as radically individuating activities; but it is a radically individuating activity in a different sense than the other two. Thinking knows no limits to dismantling the given past in quest of its meaning. Because the thinking subject withdraws from the world in this quest, thinking can never deceive him about the world around him, although Arendt never fails to remind us that it can "produce non-sense or meaninglessness."[104] The unrestrained freedom of the will also knows no limits, beyond internal consistency, to the meaning of the *enduring I* the willing subject can assemble out of the fragments of the meaning of his dismantled past, although assuredly it can be a product of self-deception and self-delusion. The activity of judging, however, immerses the judging subject in the limits of the world. Exercising my faculty of judgment does not bring into focus my relationship to myself, as do thinking and willing, but my relationship to the world as a plurality of others who are also making judgments about what I am judging.

In brief, a judgment confronts its limits in the judgments of others that carry doubt to the validity of my own judgment. If the power of thinking rests on liberating the self from a past that is given to it as the truth of its life, and the power of willing liberates the self to begin something new, then

The power of judgment rests on a potential agreement with others, and the thinking process which is active in judging something is not, like the thought processes of pure reasoning, a dialogue between me and myself, but finds itself always and primarily, even if I am quite alone in making up my mind, in an anticipated communication with others with whom I know I must finally come to some agreement. From this poten-

tial agreement judgment derives its specific validity. This means, on the one hand, that such judgment must liberate itself from the "subjective private conditions," that is, from the idiosyncrasies which naturally determine the outlook of each individual in his privacy and are legitimate as long as they are only privately held opinions, but which are not fit to enter the market place, and lack all validity in the public realm.[105]

The faculty of judgment is politically potent because it brings into focus the full meaning of Arendt's concept of *freedom.* "For Arendt," Beiner tells us, "the act of judging represents the culmination of tripartite activity of the mind because, on the one hand, it maintains the contact with 'the world of appearances' that is characteristic of 'willing,' and on the other hand it fulfills the quest for meaning that animates 'thinking.'"[106] Freedom is a concept that refers us to the full play of all of the faculties that comprise the life of the mind in a world of others.

Human beings cannot act without attempting to understand their identity as actors with an understanding that is simultaneously constitutive of the meaning of their identity. And understanding the meaning of who they are as actors is unthinkable except in terms of their similarity to and difference from others—i.e., as the member of a group. The principle is more than a function of the imperatives of language—it is also a sociological imperative. Meeting the practicalities of living means that no one can escape coordinating his actions with others in a group where individuals are bound together by a common sense of the meaning of things. Beiner quotes Arendt as pointing out that: "Common sense discloses to us the nature of the world insofar as it is a common world. . . . Judging is one, if not the most, important activity in which this sharing-the-world-with-others comes to pass."[107]

But sharing a world of the commonsense meaning of things does not mean that groups are in some way more than groups of individuals who have the power to *think, will,* and *judge.* Individuals are not welded to the group by a process of *identification* by which they transcend their own individuality, but by their activities of thinking, willing, and judging that result in the common sense of the meaning of the world that they share with each other as a practical matter and allowing them as a group to accomplish their tasks. This common sense is not a fixed constant but is always in motion as individuals instruct each other about it as they think, will, and judge.

Theoreticians who confuse thinking with prioritizing the vita contemplativa over the vita activa are fond of imagining that individuals confront the riddle of who they are as a philosophical or scientific problem. It is, however, by engaging the concrete, specific issues that appear along with the others with whom I must live that I continuously struggle to solve the riddle of my coherent identity. It is a sign that I refuse my individuality as a being with the power to think, will, and judge, when I take instruction about my judgments from those who claim to stand in the sharp light of a truth that casts the shadows in the cave where I live my life, rather than from the judgments of others who live there with me.

It is true, as Beiner points out, that for Arendt, "[h]uman judgment tends to be tragic judgment. It continually confronts a reality it can never fully master but to which it must nonetheless reconcile itself."[108] But as Beiner also points out, quoting Arendt, she also tells us that "[t]he political function of the storyteller—historian or novelist" and we would add, each individual who must constitute the meaning of his life as a story he is always ready to tell, "—is to teach acceptance of things as they are. Out of this acceptance, which can also be called truthfulness, arises the faculty of judgment."[109] The space of my *now* is a public space in which the turmoil of discourse between plural judgments takes place, each instructing the other about itself and each seeking an elusive validation from the other. What else could one call this but the "political function of the storyteller . . .?"

What Arendt calls *political* is neither a type of activity nor a set of topics defined by the interests of expert scholars. The term *political* refers us to a public space in which humans can make a livable world that can support the burden of identity that is the condition of their existence. Placing one's judgments in the midst of the turmoil of a public space of plural judgments does not erase the doubt that I can understand the meaning of myself—that is, that I can answer the question of who I am. But it makes carrying the burden of identity bearable. As Beiner points out, it is in the public space where judging takes place that doubt becomes intelligible and functional for myself:

> Without judgments by which to render our world intelligible, the space
> of appearances would simply collapse. The right of judgment is there-
> fore absolute and inalienable, for it is by constantly pronouncing judg-

ments that we are able to make sense of the world to ourselves. If we forfeited our faculty of judgment, through love or diffidence, we would be sure to lose our bearings in the world.[110]

The public space where judging takes place is where I can confront what I cannot escape—others who are the contingencies that make it impossible for me to possess myself—as others I can enlist in my continuous struggle to answer the question of who I am. In other words, in that public space, what replaces the thrilling power of a theoretically abstract truth that answers the question of who I am even before I ask it—a power whose exercise Kafka was peerless in showing makes the world unintelligible—is the sense of wonderment that I can enlist others in my struggle to become unified with myself that I continuously renew as my life. Arendt describes the full scope of what comes to me as a consciousness of myself through judging in a public space: "Plurality is the condition of human action because we are all the same, that is human, in such a way that nobody is ever the same as anyone else who ever lived, lives, or will live."[111] There is unquestionably tragedy in this discovery, but there is also "a sense of hope by which to sustain [men] in action when confronted with tragic barriers."[112]

Arendt's redefining political action in terms of the requirement imposed on all humans to judge traces out the line that Nazi totalitarianism crossed that made it the historically unique perpetrator of the Final Solution. Virtually an entire nation crossed the line under the command not to judge but to stand silent and mute before a universal truth that commanded all judgments. The self's judgment of itself as to whether its actions conform to a truth that commands them is not judging because it is not displaying one's own individual judgment in a public space that confronts the individual judgments of others. It is rather a judgment made in the private solitude of one's experience of whether one is truly being loyal to a belief given to him that promises to carry him out of the turmoil of self-doubt to that peaceful condition in which he dreams he will possess himself and the possibilities of his life.

The ultimate horror of the Final Solution was how peripheral it was, indeed even inconsequential to ordinary people to justify their participation in murder with judgments about the victims—even for those ordinary people who actually pulled triggers or released gas pellets or kept the engines running in the execution vans. What was more important, as it was to Eichmann, was for the murderer to judge his own loyalty to the command not to judge. Murder without judgment is possible only when those being murdered are refused the status of human beings who also judge, and who carry with their capacity to judge doubt into the heart of the identity of those who judge them.

Murder without judging the victim carries the possibility of assembling and putting into motion the ruthless machinery of mass murder that represented the unprecedented national policy of Nazi totalitarianism. For Arendt, the "subterranean stream of European history" prepared the way for the unprecedented by carrying away the public space of *The Political* where individuals can face each other's individual judgments. The line that separates the disappearance of The Political from the destruction of the idea of the thinking, willing, and judging individual is a tenuous one. And for Arendt, it is the disappearance of *The Political* as preparation for the crossing of this line that is the theme of *The Origins of Totalitarianism,* a theme which brings the meaning of the catastrophe of the Final Solution to bear on the experience of our own time.

Notes

1. Bhikhu C. Parekh, *Hannah Arendt and the Search for a New Political Philosophy* (Atlantic Highlands, NJ: Humanities Press, 1981), x–xi.

2. Dana R. Villa, *Arendt and Heidegger* (Princeton, NJ: Princeton University Press, 1996), 270.

3. Hannah Arendt, *The Human Condition* (Chicago: University of Chicago Press, 1958), 12.

4. Karl Joachim Weintraub, *The Value of the Individual: Self and Circumstance in Autobiography* (Chicago: University of Chicago Press, 1978), 7.

5. Hannah Arendt, *Between Past and Future,* expanded ed. (New York: Penguin Books, 1977), 146.

6. James W. Bernauer, ed., *Amor Mundi: Explorations in the Faith and Thought of Hannah Arendt* (Boston: M. Nijhoff, Kluwer Academic Publishers, 1987), 7.

7. Hannah Arendt, *On Revolution* (New York: Viking Press, 1963), 284.

8. Arendt, *Between Past and Future,* 146.

9. Arendt, *The Human Condition,* 15–16.

10. Bernauer, *Amor Mundi,* 7.

11. Arendt, *The Human Condition,* 14.

12. Matthew H. Kramer, *Legal Theory, Political Theory and Deconstruction: Against Rhadamanthus* (Bloomington: Indiana University Press, 1991), 95–96.

13. Amos Funkenstein, *Perceptions of Jewish History* (Los Angeles: University of California Press, 1993), 235.

14. Quoted in Bernauer, *Amor Mundi,* 30.

15. Arendt, *The Human Condition,* 7.

16. Quoted in Bernauer, *Amor Mundi,* 30.

17. Arendt, *The Human Condition,* 185.

18. Arendt, *The Human Condition,* 7.

19. Arendt, *Between Past and Future,* 45.

20. M. I. Finley, *The World of Odysseus* (London: Penguin Books, 1991), 22.

21. Arendt, *The Human Condition,* fn. 23.

22. Arendt, *The Human Condition,* 5.

23. Arendt, *The Human Condition,* 205.

24. Arendt, *The Human Condition,* 205.

25. Arendt, *Between Past and Future,* 46.

26. Arendt, *Between Past and Future,* 46.

27. Arendt, *Between Past and Future,* 43.

28. Finley, *The World of Odysseus,* 117.

29. Arendt, *The Human Condition,* 193–94.

30. Finley, *The World of Odysseus,* 113.

31. Finley, *The World of Odysseus,* 116–17.

32. Alvin Gouldner, *Enter Plato* (New York: Basic Books, 1965), 15.

33. Gouldner, *Enter Plato,* 15

34. Arendt, *Between Past and Future,* 47.

35. Anthony Thorlby, "Anti-Mimesis: Kafka and Wittgenstein," in *On Kafka: Semi-Centenary Perspectives,* ed. Franz Kuna (New York: Barnes and Noble, 1976), 60.

36. Hannah Arendt, *Essays in Understanding: 1930–1945* (New York: Harcourt, Brace, 1994), 80.

37. Hannah Arendt, *The Life of the Mind,* vol. 1 (New York: Harcourt, Brace, Jovanovitch, 1978), 202.

38. Arendt, *The Life of the Mind,* vol. 1, 202.

39. Arendt, *The Life of the Mind,* vol. 1, 206.

40. Arendt, *The Life of the Mind,* vol. 1, 203.

41. Arendt, *The Human Condition,* 180.

42. Arendt, *The Human Condition,* 181.

43. Cited in Arendt, *The Human Condition,* 248.

44. Arendt, *The Human Condition,* 207.

45. Arendt, *The Human Condition,* 284.

46. Arendt, *The Human Condition,* 263.

47. Quoted in Arendt, *The Human Condition,* 248.

48. Arendt, *The Human Condition,* 40.

49. Christopher Goodden, "The Great Wall of China: The Elaboration of an Intellectual Dilemma," in *On Kafka,* ed. Franz Kuna, 135.

50. Goodden, "The Great Wall of China," 132.

51. Goodden, "The Great Wall of China," 133.

52. Franz Kafka, "The Great Wall of China," in *Kafka: The Complete Stories and Parables,* ed. Nahum N. Glazer (New York: Quality Paperback Book Club, 1983), 239.

53. Goodden, "The Great Wall of China," 135.

54. Goodden, "The Great Wall of China," 136.

55. Goodden, "The Great Wall of China," 144–45.

56. Kafka, "The Great Wall of China," 244–45.

57. Arendt, *The Life of the Mind,* vol. 1, 209–10.

58. Arendt, *The Life of the Mind,* vol. 1, 209.

59. Arendt, *Essays in Understanding,* 309.

60. J. Hillis Miller, *Ariadne's Thread* (New Haven, CT: Yale University Press, 1992), 18.

61. Arendt, *The Life of the Mind,* vol. 1, 208.

62. Arendt, *The Life of the Mind,* vol. 1, 208.

63. Arendt, *The Life of the Mind,* vol. 1, 209.

64. Arendt, *The Life of the Mind,* vol. 1, 209.

65. Hannah Arendt, *The Origins of Totalitarianism,* 3d ed. (New York: Harvest/HBJ, 1968), 479.

66. Mary Warnock, *Memory* (London: Faber and Faber, 1987), 37.

67. Hannah Arendt, *Rahel Varnhagen, The Life of a Jewish Woman,* rev. ed., tr. Richard and Clara Winston (New York: Harcourt, Brace, and Jovanovitch, 1974), 4.

68. Arendt, *Essays in Understanding,* 208.

69. Timothy Brennan, "The National Longing for Form," in *Nation and Narrative,* ed. Homi K. Bhabha (London: Routledge, 1990), 44–45.

70. Arendt, *Essays in Understanding,* 16–18.

71. Hannah Arendt, "On Hannah Arendt," in *Hannah Arendt: The Recovery of the Public World,* ed. Melvyn A. Hill (New York: St. Martin's Press, 1979), 334.

72. Arendt, *The Life of the Mind,* vol. 1, 69.

73. Arendt, *The Life of the Mind,* vol. 1, 70.

74. Arendt, *The Life of the Mind,* vol. 1, 70–71.

75. Arendt, *The Life of the Mind,* vol. 1, 76–77.

76. Arendt, *The Life of the Mind,* vol. 1, 168.

77. Arendt, *The Life of the Mind,* vol. 1, 169–70.

78. Arendt, *The Life of the Mind,* vol. 1, 171.

79. Arendt, *The Life of the Mind,* vol. 1, 175.

80. Arendt, *The Life of the Mind,* vol. 1, 213.

81. J. Glenn Gray, "The Abyss of Freedom—and Hannah Arendt," in *Hannah Arendt,* ed. Melvyn A. Hill, 233.

82. Arendt, *The Life of the Mind,* vol. 1, 213.

83. Gray, "The Abyss of Freedom," 227–28.

84. Gray, "The Abyss of Freedom," 235.

85. Gray, "The Abyss of Freedom," 233.

86. Arendt, *The Life of the Mind,* vol. 1, 76–77.

87. Arendt, *The Life of the Mind,* vol. 2, 14.

88. Arendt, *The Life of the Mind,* vol. 1, 212.

89. Arendt, *The Life of the Mind,* vol. 1, 212.

90. Arendt, *The Life of the Mind,* vol. 1, 212.

91. Quoted in Elisabeth Young-Bruehl, *Hannah Arendt: For Love of the World* (New Haven, CT: Yale University Press, 1982), 452.

92. Arendt, *The Life of the Mind,* vol. 2, 196.

93. Quoted in Warnock, *Memory,* 34.

94. Arendt, *The Life of the Mind,* vol. 2, 195.

95. Arendt, *The Life of the Mind,* vol. 2, 195.

96. Arendt, *The Life of the Mind,* vol. 2, 217.

97. Quoted in Ronald Beiner, "Interpretive Essay," in *Hannah Arendt: Lectures on Kant's Political Philosophy,* ed. Ronald Beiner (Chicago: University of Chicago Press, 1989), 104.

98. Beiner, "Interpretive Essay," 105.

99. Beiner, "Interpretive Essay," 105.

100. Beiner, "Interpretive Essay," 105.

101. M. W. Jackson, "The Responsibility of Judgment and the Judgment of Responsibility," in *Hannah Arendt: Thinking, Judging, Freedom,* ed. Gisela T. Kaplan and Clive S. Kessler (Sydney: Allen and Unwin, 1989), 51.

102. Arendt, "On Hannah Arendt," 317.

103. Beiner, "Interpretive Essay," 112.

104. Arendt, *The Life of the Mind,* vol. 1, 64.

105. Arendt, *Between Past and Future,* 220.

106. Beiner, "Interpretive Essay," 144.

107. Beiner, "Interpretive Essay," 104–5.

108. Beiner, "Interpretive Essay," 143.

109. Beiner, "Interpretive Essay," 143.
110. Beiner, "Interpretive Essay," 101.
111. Arendt, *The Human Condition,* 8.
112. Beiner, "Interpretive Essay," 143.

4

The Problem of Terror

~ 1 ~

To reach the meaning of the Final Solution requires treating *judgment* as the critical constituent of the experience of being an individual. It is true, as Beiner points out, that in *The Life of the Mind* the accounts of *thinking* and *willing* "remain deficient without the promised synthesis in judging"[1] because Arendt died before transposing her lectures on Kant's political philosophy into the book. But we can glean from her lectures that *judging* synthesizes more than her accounts of the other faculties of the mind. It synthesizes the experience of being an individual agent with the capacity to begin something new. This synthetic meaning of *judging* introduces a radical perspective that adds to the unique character of Arendt's work: the possibility for experiencing individuality is contingent on occupying a space in which individuals can continuously renew their struggle to answer the question, *Who am I?*

When we consider the definition of this space the description of judging takes a peculiar tack. Arendt posits its description on the relationship between the judging individual and the world that serves as the basis for Kant's analysis of aesthetic judgments that express personal *taste*. Personal taste is an expression of individuals who position themselves as spectators of a spectacle. A judgment of personal taste in Kant, Arendt points out, quoting Kant, "arises from 'a merely contemplative pleasure or inactive delight' (*untätiges Wohlgefallen*). This 'feeling of contemplative pleasure is called taste' and the *Critique of Judgment* was originally called Critique of Taste."[2]

Arendt argues that it is wrong to treat Kant's *Critique of Judgment* as a marginal work on the question of taste, which was "a favorite topic

119

of the whole eighteenth century."[3] She points out that Kant's "final position on the French Revolution, an event that played a central role in his old age, when he waited with great impatience every day for the newspapers, was decided by this attitude of the mere spectator, of those 'who are not engaged in the game themselves' but only follow it with 'wishful, passionate participation,' which certainly did not mean, least of all for Kant, that they now wanted to make a revolution; their sympathy arose from mere 'contemplative pleasure and inactive delight.'"[4]

Judging, however, which positions the individual as a spectator observing a spectacle, suggests an antipolitical stance of indifference to a world that commands urgent action. But for Arendt it does not at all represent antipolitical indifference, because to judge something with the attitude of a spectator is not to distance oneself from taking action; it is to engage in a particular kind of action in relation to other people who are judging the same thing or event. One cannot judge as a spectator without being aware that one is viewing a spectacle that is being judged from the vantage point of other spectators. Judging is not judging without the discomforting experience that one has only a partial view of something, while others may be seeing the whole of it. Only by convincing oneself that one has an *impartial* view of something can this discomfort be relieved. Arendt looks favorably on Kant's observation that, in her terms, "*impartiality* is obtained by taking the viewpoints of others into account; impartiality is not the result of some higher standpoint that would then actually settle the dispute by being altogether above the melée."[5]

In Kant, Arendt notes, "the word 'impartiality' is not mentioned. In its stead, we find the notion that one can 'enlarge' one's own thought so as to take into account the thoughts of others."[6] We must not, however, underestimate the significance of Kant's notion of having one's thought *enlarged* by translating it too quickly into Arendt's *impartiality*. "Enlarging one's thought" emphasizes that to speak one's judgments is not only a means of engaging others to disclose who one is, but is a means of engaging oneself in the ongoing struggle to define for oneself who one is.

It is in this sense that we can say that judging is action that for Arendt, as for Kant, carries "hope," but not because she believes, as did Kant, in "the idea of progress, the hope for the future, where one judges the event according to the promise it holds for the generations to come."[7] The spectacle before the judging spectator is not the process of history, but the appearance of particular things and events. Judging is action, but it has no purpose or end beyond that of disclosing simultaneously to oneself and to others who one is as one speaks *now* about things whose appearance is common to the self and others. This action is no more than meeting the condition of being a human individual in a world of human individuals. True, judging as social discourse can result in the emergence of a world of common meanings, but it is a world that thinking, willing, and judging individuals must constantly create anew. As Villa succinctly puts it: "For Arendt it is not *agreement* that is 'an end in itself for all parties,' but *action* and *judgment.*" It is the practice of these by individuals that "gives voice to plurality—to debate, deliberation, and disagreement as well as consensus . . . what Arendt calls the 'incessant discourse' born of plurality."[8]

This notion of *incessant discourse* captures perfectly what it is that judgment synthesizes as the experience of being an individual: This experience is never one that arises from some kind of private relationship I establish with myself. Such a relationship exists but can only yield what the solitary discourse between me and myself, which defines thinking, can yield—an understanding of the continuous history of myself as a struggle to answer the question of who I am. The experience of myself as the agent who must begin that struggle anew is dependent on participating in an "incessant discourse born of plurality" that can only arise in a public space.

It is the disappearance of this space that is the subject of the story *The Origins of Totalitarianism* tells that Arendt calls the "subterranean stream of European history."[9] The underlying theme of that story is actually articulated most clearly in her subsequent book, *The Human Condition.* There, in what is surely a startling association, Arendt marks that nebulous, almost mythical historical moment we call the *origin of modernity* with the emergence of what she regards as the distinctly modern idea of *society.* Modernity originates when society emerges as a space that "devour[s] the older realms of the political and private. . . ."[10] Arendt is referring us again to the classical Greek experience, this time of the *polis:*

[A]ction is entirely dependent upon the constant presence of others. This special relationship between action and being together seems fully to justify the early translation of Aristotle's *zōon politikon* by *animal socialis*. . . . More than any elaborate theory, this unconscious substitution of the social for the political betrays the extent to which the original Greek understanding of politics had been lost. For this it is significant but not decisive that the word "social" is Roman in origin and has no equivalent in Greek language or thought. . . . It is only with the later concept of a *societas generis humani,* a "society of mankind," that the term "social" begins to acquire the general meaning of a fundamental human condition.[11]

The Greeks, of course, did not fail to realize that collective action was required to meet the exigencies of existence. For them, however, "[t]he natural, merely social companionship of the human species was considered to be a limitation imposed upon us by the needs of biological life, which are the same for the human animal as for other forms of animal life."[12] They conceived of themselves as occupying two distinctly different kinds of space, private and public:

The distinction between a private and a public sphere of life corresponds to the household and the political realms, which have existed as distinct separate entities since the rise of the ancient city–state; but the emergence of the social realm, which is neither private nor public, strictly speaking, is a relatively new phenomenon whose origin coincided with the emergence of the modern age and which found its political form in the nation–state.[13]

The private realm is where the Greeks worked to build the durable things necessary to insure the continuity of life. But building something durable was not the purpose for acting in the public realm. The public realm was the space for political action "from which everything merely necessary or useful is strictly excluded."[14] Arendt's emphasis on the relationship between the organization of the classical Greek household in a private space and the public political space of freely acting Greek citizens is not meant to represent some ideal condition that existed before a fall. It was meant to underscore the point that "[t]he realm of the *polis* . . . was the sphere of freedom, and if there was a relationship between these two spheres [the private and the public] it was a matter of course that the mastering of the necessities of life in the household was the condition of freedom for the *polis*. Under no circumstances could politics be only a means to protect society. . . ."[15]

It is, however, precisely such a notion of politics that suffuses the fabric of every modern society, whether woven out of religious beliefs, capitalist economics, or the Marxist theory of history. Modern societies command loyalty to a world where there is nothing left to see, where everything has already been identified and named, and where all that remains of individuals' experience is the urgency to act. A modern society's call for urgent action is not, however, a call for action at all in the sense of calling individuals to begin something new and extraordinary. Society demands "behavior," not action:

> It is decisive that society, on all its levels, excludes the possibility of action, which formerly was excluded from the household. Instead society expects from each of its members a certain kind of behavior, imposing innumerable and various rules, all of which tend to normalize its members, to make them behave, to exclude spontaneous action or outstanding achievement.[16]

Modern societies absorb into themselves "the life process . . . which in one form or another" they channel "into the public realm."[17] From their beginning they gave a name to the life process: It is "the assumption that men behave and do not act with respect to each other, that lies at the root of the modern science of economics, whose birth coincided with the rise of society. . . ."[18] The rise of economic science, which prescribes that individuals, because they are members of society, follow "certain patterns of behavior, so that those who do not keep the rules could be considered to be asocial or abnormal. . . ."[19] To be asocial or abnormal in modern society is not, as it once was, to have succumbed to what everybody knew were the temptations of sin, but to fail to behave in accordance with what "experts" know to be true. *Incessant discourse* ends with modernity because what can ordinary men know that is true? The modern idea of society, Arendt argues, is supported by the foundation of Cartesian doubt:

> In modern philosophy and thought, doubt occupies much the same central position as that occupied for all the centuries before by the Greek

thaumazein, the wonder at everything that is as it is. Descartes was the first to conceptualize this modern doubting, which after him became the self-evident, inaudible motor which has moved all thought, the invisible axis around which all thinking has centered. Just as from Plato and Aristotle to the modern age conceptual philosophy, in its greatest and most authentic representatives, had been the articulation of wonder, so modern philosophy since Descartes has consisted in the articulations and ramifications of doubting. . . . [M]an had been deceived so long as he had trusted that reality and truth would reveal themselves to his senses and his reason if only he remained true to what he saw with the eyes of body and mind.[20]

The profundity of Descarte's doubt is found in the divorce it forces between *Being* and *Appearance.* "If Being and Appearance part company forever, and this—as Marx once remarked—is indeed the basic assumption of all modern science, then there is nothing left to be taken upon faith; everything must be doubted."[21] When Being and Appearance became separated, the world, which Arendt states was "kept together and ruled over by common sense, the sixth and highest sense . . ." that "fit man into the reality which surrounds him . . .,"[22] was dissolved. The meaning of things became uncoupled from a commonsense world where objects appear whose identity is commonly known to everyone. No longer would it be possible to believe John Capgrave, "the early-fifteenth-century Augustinian Friar" who, Ruth Morse tells us, when he wrote "that the corpse of Henry I (who died in 1135) stank horribly . . . expected his readers to understand moral criticism. Because it had been a long-agreed proof of sanctity that the deceased holy person's body resisted decomposition so far as to smell sweet rather than to putrefy, a corpse that stank might be taken as evidence of the opposite kind of life. Not John Capgrave, but Nature herself, revealed the dead king's character."[23]

Capgrave was not reporting what we would call an empirical observation of his own or anyone else's of Henry's corpse. Obviously, he himself never saw or smelled it. But that did not matter then as it does now. We are obliged to regard Capgrave's report as an invented story, a fiction if not outright deception until proven different. But Morse observes that it was otherwise for Capgrave's listeners: "[M]edieval (and many Renaissance) readers and writers seem to have thought they could read through or across conventional styles, narrative types, and languages to a kind of prelinguistic core of truth that lay beneath."[24]

In the modern world it is not the meaning commonly associated with the appearance of things that reveals a "prelinguistic truth" about their identity; in the modern world the way things appear conceals a prelinguistic truth about the meaning of their identity. Modernity is another name for a world that replaced the one that, as Carolly Erickson points out, had a density and reality because there were narratives that gave meaning to everything and everyone that appeared or could ever appear in it. Maps were themselves such *narratives:* The "readiness to believe that real lands underlay geographical legends spurred an exploratory mentality that led the thirteenth-century Genoese to discover the Canary Islands and later to conceive a Westward voyage to Asia."[25] And lest we assume that only an ability to read gave people access to the common meaning of the identity of things and people, we should keep in mind Huizinga's observation that in the Middle Ages "[t]he bells were in daily life like good spirits, which by their familiar voices, now called upon the citizens to mourn and now to rejoice, now warned them of danger, now exhorted them to piety."[26] The sound of bells, as well as everything else that impacted on the senses, had a lexical meaning in the Middle Ages that belonged to narratives about the reality of events that told people what they must do in terms of who they were.

The idea that we can speak meaningfully about something without first questioning its appearance as to its Being is fanciful in the face of our modern definition of meaningful knowledge as *knowing the hidden truth of what things that appear really are.* When Arendt speaks of the modern world, she is speaking of a world where truth can be spoken only in an uncommon language by those who have an uncommon eye to see it: "The reason why it may be wise to distrust the political judgment of scientists *qua* scientists is not primarily their lack of 'character' . . . but precisely the fact that they move in a world where speech has lost its power. And whatever men do or know or experience can make sense only to the extent that it can be spoken about."[27]

This last, of course, is still true, but because we can no longer completely trust our normal human senses used in ordinary life to make sense of things, abstract theory has become our conduit into the hidden reality that discloses the truth of what things are. And as Arendt points out, "[w]hen the trust that things appear as they really are was gone . . . [t]he notion of 'theory' changed its meaning. It no longer meant a system of reasonably connected truths which as such had not been made but given to reason and the senses. Rather it became the modern scientific theory . . . depending for its validity not on what it 'reveals' but on whether it 'works.'"[28]

On the level of the meaning that the self has to itself, the division between *Being* and *Appearance,* which Cartesian doubt insists on, is a rift between the self and itself. Put another way: If before Descartes the motor that fired-up thought was located in the world displaying itself as a spectacle to be viewed with "admiration and wonder," then after Descartes that motor was moved from the world into the self. As Hoffman points out, Descartes made it clear that "our doubt about the reality of what we see implies the certainty of our thought of seeing."[29] For Descartes, that I exist because I have thoughts about the world is the only certainty I can have because I must doubt the reality of everything I think about. On the other side of doubt lies the certainty of truth that can be found by the only certainty left after doubting everything: the mind that thinks. As Arendt puts it:

> [T]he loss of certainty of truth ended in a new, entirely unprecedented zeal for truthfulness—as though man could afford to be a liar only so long as he was certain of the unchallengeable existence of truth and objective reality, which surely would survive and defeat all his lies. The radical change in moral standards occurring in the first century of the modern age was inspired by the needs and ideals of its most important group of men, the new scientists; and the modern cardinal virtues success, industry, and truthfulness—are at the same time the greatest virtues of modern science.[30]

If we follow Arendt, then every scientific law that represents the true nature of reality also represents the irresistible triumph of virtue. And because every modern society demands virtuous behavior from its members that conforms to the various species of scientific reason—sociological, economic, psychological, biological, medical, etc.—that define the *life processes* that every society presumably guarantees and protects, modern societies can virtually be called *scientific societies.* Every modern individual is in a perpetual state of being told a hidden truth about himself that places him in a perpetual condition of being like a patient who needs moral therapy. It is as if understanding the self's ability to understand the meaning of itself by thinking toward itself is monopolized by the scientific project of placing under human control the forces, often implied to be demonic, that are presumed to define the true being of everything, including the self, that simply appears in the world.

But Arendt is not saying that modernity, by voiding the world of a public space that the Greeks once conceived was the realm for acting, has erased the human capacity to think toward the meaning of the self. What she is saying is something equally foreboding: Where there is no public space for acting but only the public space of society identified as the world for behaving, the answer to the question, *Who am I?*, becomes located in solitary private relationships that individuals can have with themselves. "We call private today," Arendt observes, "a sphere of intimacy whose beginnings we may be able to trace back to late Roman, though hardly to any period of Greek antiquity, but whose peculiar manifoldness and variety were certainly unknown to any period prior to the modern age."[31] Arendt is not referring to the intimacy of love so carefully cultivated in the Middle Ages. She is referring to "the modern discovery of intimacy [that] seems a flight from the whole outer world into the inner subjectivity of the individual. . . ."[32]

It is undoubtedly true that in our age more than any other, as Weintraub remarks, "we are captivated by an uncanny sense that each of us constitutes one irreplaceable human form, and we perceive a noble life-task in the cultivation of our individuality, our ineffable self."[33] Cultivating the "ineffable self" is a project that Rousseau was among the first to discover. Rousseau, Arendt tells us, "arrived at his discovery through a rebellion not against the oppression of the state but against society's unbearable perversion of the human heart, its intrusion upon an innermost region in man which until then had needed no special protection."[34] By our own time, the function of society had evolved "to shelter the intimate [that] was discovered as the opposite not of the political sphere but of the social. . . ."[35]

The idea of society evolved along the axis of a new distinction between an *inner* and *outer* reality that replaced the older medieval distinction between *visible* and *invisible*. This applied to the question of an individual's identity. The modern individual can be said to actually embrace two identities: a *virtual* and an *actual*, which correspond to a public and private identity, respectively, located in outer and inner spheres of reality. The coherency of the public identity is rarely in question because, displayed to the world, its coherency is shaped to meet the demands of the world. It is, however, the private identity whose coherency must meet the demands of the self that is the focus of an individual's continuing struggle to answer the question, *Who am I?* And this struggle for individuals in the modern age is pursued through intimate relations the self cultivates with its inner life of emotions, moods, and feelings. This private struggle that public life is expected to shelter and protect takes place in an inner space, located nowhere in the world, that we seem capable of describing only as our ineffable soul.

Arendt does not put a small value on what she calls "the human scale of emotions and private feelings."[36] She insists, however, that pursuing intimate relations with them cannot yield answers to the question, *Who am I?* Such relations "will always come to pass at the expense of the assurance of the reality of the world and men."[37] It is inconceivable that a minded, symbol-using being who must represent who he is by speaking about himself can answer the question of who he is, to himself or another, by using the metaphors and analogies expressive of emotions and feelings that language supplies but that always miss the mark. "[I]n the region of the inner self [there] is . . . not an image whose permanence can be beheld and contemplated, but, on the contrary, the constant movement of sensual perceptions and the no less constantly moving activity of the mind."[38] In protecting and sheltering the individual's struggle with his identity that is located in the solitude of cultivating intimate relations with his own feelings and emotions, society can only protect a struggle with the "ineffable self."

Where the struggle to answer the question, *Who am I?*, is with an ineffable self, the struggle has the potential to become a nightmare. What we almost invariably experience behind what cannot be spoken—behind what cannot be displayed to others through speech that simultaneously constitutes the meaning of the self to itself—is a truly uncanny terror. Erving Goffman makes the sociological observation that "[t]he Greeks, who were apparently strong on visual aids, originated the term *stigma* to refer to bodily signs designed to expose something unusual and bad about the moral status of the signifier."[39] He also makes the trenchant observation that using stigmata to identify people must rebound on those using them: "The stigmatized and the normal are part of each other; if one can prove vulnerable, it must be expected that the other can too. For in imputing identities to individuals, discreditable or not, the wider social setting and its inhabitants have in a way compromised themselves; they have set themselves up to being proven the fool."[40] Goffman, from his discussion that follows on the phenomenon of *passing,* seems to mean primarily that one can be vulnerable to being the fool for making an error in identifying, or failing to identify, a stigma.

But there is a more horrific sense of that to which the stigmatizer himself is vulnerable than being a fool. If the stigma lies in some "reality" below the surface of the appearance of the stigmatized, in some irremediable "stain" in his blood, for example, then the stigmatizer is vulnerable to some secret stain that would change him from a human being to something else without changing his appearance. Nightmares are most terrifying at the moment when one awakes in the solitude of still clinging to the dream. In effect, when I no longer occupy a place in a commonsense world that confirms everyone's appearance to me as human like myself as that world confirms my appearance to others, I stand alone with myself, vulnerable to an uncanny terror, confronting the question of who I really am by cultivating my ineffable self in a solitary relationship with myself. To avoid drowning in this terror means that individuals must be able to answer the question of who they are by telling a story about themselves that gives them the certainty that they are human beings. What better story can there be than one that displays me to myself and others as a member of this group or this society that epitomizes the characteristics that undoubtedly define being a true human being, as opposed to being like those in that group or society who display characteristics that cannot escape the doubt that they are human like me?

And yet it is no simple matter, in a world where the sciences mandated to speak the truth are also designed to doubt their certainties, to find something to cling to that transcends personal identity in a condition durable enough to resist the doubt penetrating it. It takes a certain blindness to how the experience of being an individual depends on a space in which one *acts* rather than *behaves. The Origins of Totalitarianism* is a peculiar history because the story it tells is a remarkable one in which *modernity* is another name for the substitution of a space called *society,* whose form may change but whose substance seems timeless and eternal, for that ephemeral space that supports the burden of individuality.

The starting point for Arendt's story of modernity is the conventional one of the revolutionary call for equality before the law for all men. The cry that all men are equal was not, of course, born with modernity. What *was* born was the call for men to escape the rigid social order grounded in church doctrine and authority. Accomplishing this escape meant shifting the ground for the principle of equality from the condition created and guaranteed by God when He judged every man equally at the time of his death to the right each man had to be judged equally before the laws of society. If, once God had commanded all men to see each man as his equal, because death was the common fate of everyone, modernity was born with society authorizing that command in the name of being the sovereign realm of the world. Arendt sees the enduring power of this principle in the history of modernity in the explosive Dreyfus affair when "[t]he doctrine of equality before the law was still so firmly implanted in the conscience of the civilized world that a single miscarriage of justice could provoke public indignation from Moscow to New York."[41]

But if Arendt's starting point is a conventional one, the story she tells is not. Modernity is a story, she tells us, about the "perversion of equality from a political into a social concept [that] is all the more dangerous when a society leaves but little space for special groups and individuals. . . ."[42] With God as the sovereign of the world, no explanation was needed for the equality that existed between people whose common destiny was death. The modern concept of society opened this certainty to doubt in the form of the question, *To whom does the principle of equality apply?*—a question that proved to be applicable by the questioner to himself. The question arose because modernity arose with the nation–state as the synonym for society, constituting a dangerous perversion of equality because, as Arendt states it, "equality demands that I recognize each and every individual as my equal. . . ." Equality can exist only where there is a space that makes it possible for individuals to experience themselves as individuals. Without this space, "the conflicts between different groups, which for reasons of their own are reluctant to grant each other this basic equality, take on such terribly cruel forms."[43]

The story of this dangerous perversion of equality that Arendt tells is a complex one consisting of two intertangled parts: the story of the Jews who became vulnerable to being defined by the nation as a problem calling for a solution when they lost the protection of the state, and the story of the ordinary citizen's experience of individuality that became vulnerable to a fictional world of terror.

~ **2** ~

Arendt's phrasing that groups refuse each other basic equality "for reasons of their own" is vague enough to invite misreading the story as the conventional one of various forms of nationalist anti-Semitism victimizing the Jews. It is a conventional observation that "[t]he series of emancipation edicts which slowly and hesitantly followed the French edict of 1792 had been preceded and were accompanied by an equivocal attitude toward its Jewish inhabitants,"[44] and that constituting the Jews as a special group without full equality prevailed in European societies throughout the nineteenth and twentieth centuries.

But the direction that Arendt's story takes departs from the conventional when she asserts that "[t]here is no doubt that the nation–state's interest in preserving the Jews as a special group . . . coincided with the Jewish interest in self-preservation and group survival."[45] In effect, Arendt is entering the prolific, long-standing efforts to illuminate the origins and nature of the modern nation–state with its concomitant nationalist ideologies, with the proposition that the Jews were not simply a problem for the nation–state, but the nation–state was also problem for the Jews. Illuminating the questions that surround the origin and nature of the modern nation–state requires attending to the reciprocally equivocal relationship the Jews had with it.

What has always been the problem in understanding the origins of the modern nation–state has been the fervent, some say fanatical, nationalistic feelings that have been there from its beginning. Focusing on the French Revolution, which Geoffrey Best has called "the apotheosis of the nation–state within the modern theory and practice of nationalism,"[46] O'Brien refuses the consoling thesis, embraced by many, that "nationalism, like the Terror" is "a revolutionary distortion not merely a deviation from the true standards of the Enlightenment . . . an actual usurpation by essentially the same forces that Voltaire and his friends had fought."[47]

While it is true that Voltaire and his friends were concerned that societies bestow on its citizens the universal blessings of civilization by divorcing reason from passion and belief from desire rather than bestow on them the particular blessings of a particular nationhood, this O'Brien implies misses the role they played in the origin of the nation–state: "The *philosophes* hoped to rid the world of fanaticism, but what they actually seemed to have done is to have provided fanaticism with a new deity. . . . [B]y the second half of the eighteenth century there was a yawning emotional void, left by the discredited notions of God and king. And the idea of the nation, *la patrie,* was beginning to fill the void."[48]

O'Brien's argument joins him with those who argue that nationalist sentiments and ideologies did not follow the French Revolution, thereby infecting its Enlightenment ideals, but preceded it as its possibility. Balibar, for example, observes that understanding the phenomenon of bringing together diverse populations into a unified "people . . . subject to a common law" requires

> In every case . . . a model of their unity [that] must "anticipate" that constitution: the process of unification . . . must at one and the same time be a mass phenomenon and a phenomenon of individuation, must effect an "interpellation of individuals as subjects" (Althusser) which is much more potent than the mere inculcation of political values or rather one that integrates this inculcation into a more elementary process (which we may term "primary") of fixation of the affects of love and hate and representation of the "self."[49]

Invoking the potency of such "elementary processes" at the individual level without resorting to simplistic formulas of causal determinism is in accord with Arendt's concept of the modern nation–state as a synonym for the modern idea of society. Such an idea of society, states Arendt, "always demands that its members act as though they were members of one enormous family which has only one opinion and one interest."[50] Arendt's trope that modern society is like a family is not meant to support the psychological image, fashionable since

Rousseau, that society, where we begin, is like a rich medium in which we grow into ourselves as our individuality matures. Arendt's trope implies rather that modern society presents itself to us, to borrow Liah Greenfield's apt terminology, as a space "[w]e live *in,* in much the same manner as fish live in water."[51]

The idea of the modern nation–state arises as the invocation of individual identity based on a principle of dependency: You can have no experience of being an individual without identifying with the shelter and protection it affords. And the mark of that sheltering and protection is the mythologizing, in nationalist ideologies, the primal narcissism that irremediably ties family members to each other: People belong together who can see themselves in each other.

The emergence of the nation–state with citizens equal under the law redefined the social geography that located and identified the apparent divisions within it. Fueled by the revolutionary ardor of *progress,* traditional landmarks were replaced by new ones. In this respect Gay observes that "[i]t is . . . anything but accidental that the traditional static names for social divisions—'estates' or, more graphic, 'orders,' or, more graphic still, *Stände*—gave way, in the nineteenth century, to names appropriate to a divided society open to the prospect of improvement: 'classes,' 'parties,' or, late in the century, 'interest groups.'"[52] The revolution in the self-consciousness of social identity evolved, of course, unevenly throughout enlightened Europe. But what emerged throughout enlightened Europe was the transposition of the pattern of earlier ages into the concept of a pattern indigenous to all natural things, of which society was one. The image of society is the image of what is natural, and to be without its protection and shelter is to be "outside nature itself: *hors nature,*" which O'Brien points out was a favorite metaphor of the French revolutionists.[53]

The trope of the nation as "one enormous family," Arendt implies, states as well the terms in which Jews understood their history and identity out of which they fashioned their response to the newly emerging nation–states. In her preface to Part One, "Antisemitism," in the revised version of *The Origins of Totalitarianism,* Arendt states what amounts to her discovery, seventeen years after the book was originally published, that her understanding of the terms in which the Jews responded to the modern nation–state was consonant with a just-published work of the historian Jacob Katz.[54] The primary reason Arendt was attracted to Katz's work was that, like herself, he did not treat anti-Semitism as if it were like a force of nature that carried Jewish history in Europe to its tragic destiny.

Anti-Semitism, defined in the familiar racial terms used by the Nazis, was not identical to the antagonism between Jews and non-Jews that marks their pre-Nazi European history. Understanding the history of this antagonism requires understanding, in Katz's terms, that "[t]he relationship between Jews and Gentiles is at all times a reciprocal one. The behaviour of the Jews towards their neighbors is conditioned by the behaviour of the latter towards them, and vice versa. . . . Every attitude of the Jew towards the non-Jew has its counterpart in a similar attitude of the Gentile towards the Jew."[55] And the attitude of Jews, who were indeed, as Arendt put it, "a people without a government, without a country and"—at least for a German intellectual who would never deign to speak Yiddish—"without a language,"[56] was nevertheless grounded in a historical sense of being a people of a nation bound together by a common eternal substance that was the foundation for the claim to a Jewish identity.

Arendt saw that the essential theme in Katz, for which the specific history of Jewish–Gentile relations during the Diaspora was a variation, was their survival as a people who were, Katz points out, "a 'national' as well as religious minority."[57] This meant, for Arendt, extrapolating from Katz, that while the history of the relations between Jews and Gentiles in the Diaspora is as complex as any history, little of it can make sense without seeing that what was at stake for Jews at every moment was their consciousness of being members of a dispersed nation.

This self-consciousness took a particular turn in the grim catastrophes that marked the centuries from the fifteenth to the end of the sixteenth that included the expulsion of Jews from Spain, France, and Germany, their enforced ghettoization, and massacres in Poland. It was then, Arendt points out, quoting Katz, that Jewish–Gentile relations hit an "all time low," and "Jewish 'indifference to conditions and events in the outside world' was at an all time high, and Judaism became 'more than ever a closed system of thought'"[58] It was then that Jews came to think of their difference from Gentiles, Katz points out, as "fundamentally not one of creed and faith, but one of inner nature.

The difference between the Jewish way of life and destiny, and the life and destiny of other nations, was not the result of Jewish acceptance of the *Torah,* as is clearly suggested by tradition; but rather the fact that the Jewish people accepted the *Torah* was itself the result of their unique nature."[59]

Jews who faced the emerging modern nation–state were the inheritors of a notable reversal in the terms by which they identified themselves as a people with a special character. They were no longer a people God chose, for reasons of his own, to believe in Him and obey His laws; they were now God's chosen people because He could choose no other. It is this belief in themselves, Arendt wrote Gershom Scholem, that she found so "shocking" in the Jews when she heard it from an anonymous "political personality" during her time in Jerusalem. It was a belief that enabled Jews to cope with their own secularizing tendencies in a world that was becoming secular, while remaining committed as firmly as ever to preserving their traditional and eternal communal bond.

Arendt divides the history of modernity into two periods in terms of different historical circumstances facing the Jews in the European Diaspora: a period from the French Revolution to the beginning of imperialism in the latter part of the nineteenth century, which then began the period ending in the Nazi catastrophe. The first period

> Brought with it the granting of privileges which up to then had been necessary only for court Jews, to the larger wealthy class, which had managed to settle in the more important urban and financial centers in the eighteenth century. Finally emancipation was granted in all full fledged nation–states and withheld only in those countries where Jews, because of their numbers and the general backwardness of those regions, had not been able to organize themselves into a special separate group whose economic function was financial support for their government.[60]

It is Arendt's contention that the relationship between premodern monarchical governments and the Jews, based on the "always influential position of court Jews who financed state affairs and handled the financial transactions of their princes,"[61] was not only carried over by the modern state, but strengthened during this period: "Only the combined wealth of the wealthier strata of Western and Central European Jewry, which they entrusted to some prominent Jewish bankers for such purposes, could suffice to meet the new enlarged governmental needs."[62] This established for the Jews a continuity of the tradition, in Katz's terms, of seeking "the protection of the holders of political power" that became formalized "from the thirteenth century onwards [when] the form that this protection assumed was the explicit definition of the Jews as being the 'king's serfs,' *servi camerae.*"[63]

While the modern state emerged with an interest in protecting the Jews, Jews never achieved genuine social and economic equality. The door, however, was open for bourgeois Jews to be in the forefront of Jewish efforts to become integrated into the new nation. But this integration was equivocal, because the idea of full political and social integration for the Jews was equivocal for both the nation and the Jews in different ways. People had, to use Arendt's apt term, a "peculiar attraction to Jews" combined with a "social resentment toward them."[64] Only exceptional Jews were socially acceptable, while at the same time exceptional Jews were seen as part of a separate Jewish community. In a significant way, Jews were caught in a classic double-bind:

> Society, confronted with political, economic, and legal equality for Jews, made it quite clear that none of its classes was prepared to grant them social equality, and that only exceptions from the Jewish people would be received. Jews who heard the strange compliment that they were exceptions, exceptional Jews, knew quite well that it was this very ambiguity—that they were Jews and yet presumably not *like* Jews—which opened the doors of society to them. If they desired this kind of intercourse, they tried therefore, "to be Jews and yet not to be Jews."[65]

We should not assume, however, that the Jews' ambiguous response was solely due to an ambiguous definition imposed on them. In this regard German Jews can serve as the exemplary case. Marion Kaplan, who studied German-Jewish bourgeois women in the nineteenth-century Jewish family in order to correct historians' "inadvertent" overestimation of "both the desire of Jews to assimilate and even their capacity to do so,"[66] found that "Jewish women wove intricate and complicated patterns in designing their environments, choosing from modern bourgeois practice and traditional familial and communal customs. Paradoxically for historians, but perfectly consistently and reasonably for themselves, they were agents of acculturation and tradition, of integration and apartness."[67] In more general terms Kaplan tells us that "German Jews acculturated to German society, but they did not 'assimilate,' nor did most ever intend to do so."[68]

Jews did not intend to exchange being Jewish for being German, the condition for assimilation that Germans at once set for them and simultaneously made clear was not to be permitted. Bourgeois Jews sustained a continuity with their Jewish identity by utilizing the private space of the family that the bourgeois class in general valued for the cultivation of the self. The boundary between private and public identities served as a way for bourgeois Jews to adapt to the modern world.

It is, of course, impossible not to judge this adaptive mode as a disastrous adaptation from the standpoint of the subsequent events in Nazi Germany and, for that matter, throughout Europe. But precisely on what grounds? Arendt's answer is that for "[t]he majority of assimilated Jews" who "lived in a twilight of favor and misfortune and knew with certainty only that both success and failure were inextricably connected with the fact that they were Jews . . . the Jewish question had lost once and for all, all political significance. . . . The adage, 'a man in the street and a Jew at home,' was bitterly realized: political problems were distorted to the point of pure perversion when Jews tried to solve them by means of inner experience and private emotions."[69] As stressful on themselves as was Jews' conformity to the dehumanizing demands made on them as the conditions for social acceptance, Arendt's answer accents their political naiveté:

> Had the Jews been bourgeois in the ordinary sense of the word, they might have gauged correctly the tremendous power-possibilities of their new functions, and at least have tried to play that fictitious role of a secret world power which makes and unmakes governments, which antisemites assigned to them anyway. Nothing, however, could be farther from the truth. The Jews, without knowledge of or interest in power, never thought of exercising more than mild pressure for minor purposes of self defense.[70]

Arendt's tone of bitter recrimination conveyed by this assessment of Jewish political blindness is somewhat misguided. By her own account, up until the last three decades of the nineteenth century, which historians including Arendt regard as the "long century" ending with World

War I, the bourgeois class in general, not just bourgeois Jews, failed to correctly gauge their power possibilities. It was a period "adequately described as a 'Golden Age of Security' because . . . [s]ide by side, and apparently with equal stability, an anachronistic despotism in Russia, a corrupt bureaucracy in Austria, a stupid militarism in Germany and a half-hearted Republic in continual crisis in France—all of them still under the shadow of the world-wide power of the British Empire—managed to carry on."[71]

What was being carried on was a tremendous economic and industrial growth, which held the bourgeois class in thrall, believing that "[p]ower was . . . synonymous with economic capacity. . . ." What was waiting to be discovered about power, by both Jews and Gentiles but with markedly different consequences, was that "economic and industrial capacity are only its modern prerequisites. In a sense, economic power could bring governments to heel because they had the same faith in economics as the plain businessman who had somehow convinced them that the state's means of violence had to be used exclusively for protection of business interests and national property."[72]

And that is precisely what happened, ushering in the second part of the nineteenth century, confronting Jews with their delusion about having been part of a Golden Age of Security: When "[t]he growing influence of big business on the state" made the state's special protection of the Jews superfluous and "the state's declining need for Jewish services threatened the Jewish banker with extinction,"[73] Jews became visible in a way that mobilized anti-Semitic attitudes. As the functions performed by the Jews for the state declined, "[a]ntisemitism reached its climax when Jews . . . were left with nothing but their wealth" and the visibility and prominence it accorded them that defined them for anti-Semites as parasitic pariahs who fed off the nation without contributing to it. The problem for the Jews, as Arendt puts it, was that "wealth without visible function is . . . intolerable because nobody can understand why it should be tolerated."[74]

~ **3** ~

The loss of the state's protection of the Jews with its concomitant upsurge of anti-Semitism corresponds with the advent of the imperialist period in Europe that lasted until World War I began, marking the end of the "long" nineteenth century. This is a period for Arendt that represents "an almost complete break in the continuous flow of Western history as we had known it for more than two thousand years."[75] The qualifier "almost" refers us, of course, to the period's restoration of the ancient idea of *empire.* "What is the content of the idea of empire?," Manent asks. "It is the bringing together of all the known world, of the *orbis terrarum,* under a unique power. The idea of empire does not refer primarily to the conquering zeal of a few individuals. . . . It corresponds instead to men's unity, to the universality of human nature, which wants to be recognized and addressed by a unique power. It is a *natural* political idea."[76]

This idea of empire, however, can be thought of as a "complete break" within the relatively short history of the modern nation–states, who restored it by shifting "from localized, limited, and therefore predictable goals of national interest to the limitless pursuit of power after power that could roam and lay waste the whole globe with no certain nationally and territorial prescribed purpose and hence no predictable direction."[77] It is true that expanding emigration, trade, and colonization had been British policy, to cite one prime example, long before the imperialist period began, but political expansion, in the sense of establishing political authority over a foreign people, became an ambition when it dominated the field of international relations, with African expansion as the most blatant example of the exercise of limitless power.

For the first three-quarters of the nineteenth century a Deist mechanistic view of a static world prevailed to give direction to the political life of nations as the pursuit of a "balance of power." Gulick tells us that "[w]riters on the balance of power have repeatedly stressed the common ground of culture in European states. They have pointed out that in addition to proximity, which undergirds a balancing system, there is a conception of a common destiny, a conception of a certain unity in spite of wars and differences."[78] For the first three-quarters of the nineteenth century, Europe, emerging from Bonaparte's shadow, thought of itself as a family of nations that made up a system of states that had equal rights to protect their independence and pursue policies of free trade. Their collective ambition was to sustain a balance of power through various alliances as well as limited wars "aimed at the survival of the state system and regarded . . . as a means of preventing the break-down of that system."[79]

By the end of the century the ambition of nations was to *expand* their power over one another, not to preserve a balance of power between them. The nations that were carving up Africa were not opening a continent to free trade, but building colonial empires. What had once been unthinkable—the possession of colonies deemed to be expensive interferences with the liberal economic doctrine of free trade that ostensibly made the world of nations work—had become the great ambition of power-hungry, competing nation–states. Leopold of Belgium, arguably the most aggressive competitor of them all, who ruled under the state motto, Wesseling ironically points out, "'L'Union fait la Force'—'Unity is strength'. . . himself lived more in accord with words taken from Schiller's *Wilhelm Tell:* 'Der Starke ist am mächtigsten allein'—'The strong is mightiest alone.'"[80]

Arendt is categorical in her judgment of the bourgeoisie's ability to win major victories in its struggle to control the state's instruments of power, thereby reshaping the nation's image of itself: It "could only destroy the political body of the nation–state."[81] At one time the instruments of power were controlled by law that unified the nation's different social classes into a political body, but "[t]he first consequence of power export was that the state's instruments of violence, the police and the army, which in the framework of the nation existed beside, and were controlled by, other national institutions, were separated from this body and promoted to the position of national representatives in uncivilized or weak countries."[82]

Power, which had once been conceived of as a finite, measurable force available to the state for limited and controlled purposes, had now become a purpose to be pursued for the sake of the existence of the nation and the state. We can say that the bourgeoisie had reversed the ancient aristocratic rule that money accrued to power, and knew by that reversal that they were blurring the distinction between the accumulation of money and power. In the imperialist period, Arendt points out that "power can be thought of as the never-ending, self-feeding motor of all political action that corresponds to the legendary unending accumulation of money that begets money." And "power left to itself can achieve nothing but more power, and violence administered for power's (and not for law's) sake turns into a destructive principle that will not stop until there is nothing left to violate."[83] This is precisely what Hobsbawm sees exemplified by World War I:

> Why . . . was the First World War waged by the leading powers on both sides as a zero-sum game, i.e., as a war which could only be totally won or totally lost? The reason was that this war, unlike earlier wars, which were typically waged for limited and specifiable objects, was waged for unlimited ends. In the Age of Empire, politics and economics had fused. International political rivalry was modelled on economic growth and competition, but the characteristic feature of this was precisely that it had no limit. . . . On paper no doubt compromise was possible on this or that point of the almost megalomaniac "war aims" which both sides formulated as soon as war had broken out, but in practice the only war aim that counted was total victory: what in the Second World War came to be called "unconditional surrender."[84]

The "fusion" of politics and economics, to use Hobsbawm's terms, in the imperialist period points to another fusion that could be said to have been apotheosized by World War I: a blind loyalty fused to the individual's idea of belonging to a nation. Loyalty to the collectivity into which individuals are born has always been loyalty to what individuals can cling to as the certainty of their identity. But the imperialist nation–state emerged as a seamless space that, by encompassing what it defined in economic terms as the processes of life itself, put at stake with its demands for loyalty the survival of every individual who received its gift of identity. Fusing economics and politics, the imperialist state no longer saw itself in the image of a dispassionate arbiter of the often-conflicting interests of the different social classes that made up the body of the nation. Now the state found a passion as the sole provider of protection from the worst terror that lay in wait for the body of the nation: to become impoverished. Only the power of the state could hold at bay the abject state of poverty.

But poverty and the fear of poverty are only the entering wedge for a greater terror. "Poverty is more than deprivation," Arendt points out, "it is a state of constant want and acute misery whose ignominy consists in its dehumanizing force; poverty is abject because it puts men under the absolute dictate of their bodies, that is under the absolute dictate of necessity as all men know it from their most intimate experience and outside all speculations."[85] The fear of poverty had become the threat to the idea of freedom, linked not to political categories but to the dream of a rich and fat nation. Without the power of the state there was only the terror of being an abject nothing.

The bourgeois ideology in the age of imperialism had caught up to Thomas Hobbes, whom Arendt calls "the only great philosopher to whom the bourgeoisie can rightly and exclusively lay claim, even if his principles were not recognized by the bourgeois class for a long time."[86] There are two reasons she offers for calling Hobbes the philosopher of the bourgeoisie: He was "the only great thinker who ever attempted to derive public good from private interest and who, for the sake of private good, conceived and outlined a Commonwealth whose basis and ultimate end is accumulation of power."[87] Neither one of these by itself, but only the two in combination, of course, makes Hobbes unique:

> Hobbes points out that in the struggle for power, as in their native capacities for power, all men are equal; for the equality of men is based on the fact that each has by nature enough power to kill another. Weakness can be compensated for by guile. Their equality as potential murderers places all men in the same insecurity, from which arises the need for a state. The *raison d'être* of the state is the need for some security of the individual, who feels himself menaced by all his fellow men.[88]

Hobbes was depicting "the features of man according to the needs of the Leviathan . . ." that was his "plan for a body politic best fitted for this power thirsty animal. . . . This new body politic was conceived for the benefit of the new bourgeois society as it emerged in the seventeenth century. . . . The Commonwealth is based on the delegation of power, and not of rights."[89]

The delegation of power to the state was originally justified by what Hirschman points out became the "major tenet of 19th century liberalism and . . . a central construct of economic theory"[90]: The freedom of everyone to pursue their private economic interests, however defined, which, because of the Invisible Hand that governs economic processes, can only bring about great public good. Up until the imperialist period the bourgeoisie were only too glad to concede the existence of professional politicians, because the final solution to the social question of poverty was, to use Hirschman's terms, "bestowed on money making . . ." with its "*positive* and *curative* [Hirschman's italics] connotation. . . ."[91]

The imperialist period, however, moved the notion of curing poverty away from the individualized processes of making money that would be guaranteed by the power of the state to ensure a balance of power within and between social classes and nations. The European powers did not carve up the body of Africa in the name of solving the social problem of poverty, but in the name of the tautological delirium of money chasing money that was indistinguishable from power chasing power because winning was chasing survival, which chased winning. Winning the battle to expand nation into empire was everything, and winning what Kipling called "The Great Game" that would be finished "only when everyone is dead . . . [n]ot before"[92] necessitated dissolving the idea that power had limiting boundaries, while reconfiguring the boundaries between leaders and the led.

Arendt inevitably sees Cecil Rhodes, with his twin apothegms, "Expansion is everything" and "I would annex the planets if I could," as the consummate player of the game. Rhodes's vision is not the same as the "sainted" Livingstone's, for whom the three "C's"—commerce, Christianity, and civilization—would finally solve the problem of Africa and the Africans, but the appetite is the same: To unify everything in the name of the law that governs everything that lives in the universe. Rhodes could and did express his appetites publicly, but it was clear to everyone who lionized him that only those with exceptional character could understand and execute what is necessary to meet a call to destiny.

In one of his numerous Last Wills and Testaments that he was apparently addicted to writing, he left most of his fortune to Lord Rothschild, a supporter and ally of his, with the proviso that he "use the money in order to establish a secret order, the Society of the Elect for the Good of Empire . . . to be modeled on the Society of Jesus."[93] This was simply an elaboration of what had already been set in motion, thanks to Rhodes himself, as well as others: the division between the state and those who delegate power to it being solidified as a boundary between an exceptional elite capable of using power to realize a vision that was both nationalistic and transcendent in content and ordinary people whom they must lead. Arendt cites the British example: "The imperialists had always been deeply resentful that the government of India should have 'to justify its existence and its policy before public opinion in England'; this control . . . made it impossible to proceed to . . . measures of 'administrative massacres.'. . ."[94] Those who must be led must be led in secrecy, because ordinary people are an obstacle to doing what is necessary since they have only timid visions limited by their ordinariness to horizons that do not extend to limitless greatness. "What imperialists actually wanted," Arendt remarks, "was expansion of political power without the foundation of a body politic."[95] Kipling's Great Game was a game shrouded in secrecy, run by a state bureaucracy. Again, for Arendt, the British provided the model: What was needed to rule a foreign people who were mere "stepping-stones in an expansion limited only by the size of the earth"[96] was an

> [I]nformal influence . . . preferable to a well-defined policy because it could be altered at a moment's notice and did not necessarily involve the home government in case of difficulties. It required a highly trained, highly reliable staff whose loyalty and patriotism were not connected with personal ambition or vanity or who would even be required to renounce the human aspiration of having their names connected with their achievements. Their greatest passion would have to be for secrecy, . . . for a role behind the scenes; their greatest contempt would be directed at publicity and people who love it.[97]

That all of this is evocative of certain themes that animated Nazi totalitarianism does not imply that Arendt is drawing a causal relationship between the imperialist and Nazi periods. She is telling us rather, as she has repeatedly, that a world exists for humans because what appears to them is conceptually organized into meanings and values that mediate action. Meanings make action possible, and the issue Arendt persists in facing is not that of predicting actions, but of making them intelligible. And an action, as Taylor points out, is intelligible "only in virtue of its having a certain meaning. . . ."[98]

Because we live in cultures that are significative systems, the intelligibility of our actions to ourselves and others change over time because cultures change over time. Changes in meanings build on each other, but not because an outside force acts on them to propel action in a predetermined direction. The system of meanings that exists at any given time is not a moment in a unified causal process but part of a "crystallizing" structure, to use Arendt's own term,[99] with all of the additions, subtractions, and divisions that create forms that defy prediction. That Nazi totalitarianism was unique in history does not mean that it sprang up *suis generis* out of nothing. It is only when we can understand the way European nations experienced themselves and the world during the imperialist period can we describe the line the Nazis crossed into the Final Solution that made their actions intelligible but not predictable.

In this regard, the most apparent theme in the imperialist period was the cool indifference as well as overt support of ordinary citizens to the brutality and large-scale murder of people being colonized in the name of their "pacification." It was the imperialist period that saw the discourse over Darwin's work move from man's relationship to God and nature to the life of the nation struggling to attain the power to achieve a unified wholeness that would testify to its destiny as the fittest and worthiest to survive. Arendt sees the national support, during the imperialist period, for egregious cruelty to "racially inferior" peoples signifying the political alienation of the ordinary citizen. Arendt uses the term *mass man* to describe the emergence and functioning of the politically alienated. Not so long ago the term was a venerable one in social studies but since then its use has diminished; however, the phenomenon to which it referred remains valid.

The concept of *mass man* has a particular meaning for Arendt that departs from what Giner has criticized as "a mass interpretation of modern society [that] has been accompanied by the development of a notion that is, essentially, the negative counterpart to the liberal theory of the individual. The opposite of a free, rational, individualistic man is not the member of the primeval tribe or horde; it is mass man. . . . He is thus a modern barbarian who, unlike his historical predecessors, does not threaten civilization from the outside, but insidiously lurks in its very midst, forever eroding its delicate web."[100] For Arendt, while "masses are not held together by a consciousness of common interest and they lack that specific class articulateness which is expressed in determined, limited, obtainable goals," the term, she warns us, is a term not to be confused with a mob. *Mass men* refers us to individuals whose loyalty to the nation allows them to cling to a certainty of their identity. It is what they cling to that characterizes them as *mass men*. While mobs are temporary phenomena, masses can be permanent fixtures in a society that suffers from the breakdown of a "bourgeois-dominated class society."[101]

To begin explicating this breakdown in psychological terms, we can turn to Colley's study of the problem of "the forging of the British nation." Colley concludes that the emergence of "mass allegiance on the one hand and the invention of Britishness on the other . . ." was due to the succession of wars between Britain and France between 1689 and 1815.[102] She compellingly argues that the forging of the unified nation of Great Britain illustrates the general point that "men and women decide who they are by reference to who and what they are not. Once confronted with an obviously alien 'Them,' an otherwise diverse community can become a reassuring or merely desperate 'Us.'"[103] However, she also offers in passing a significant caveat: "I am not suggesting for one moment that the growing sense of Britishness in this period supplanted and obliterated other loyalties. It did not. Identities are not like hats. Human beings can and do put on several at a time. . . . Britishness was superimposed over an array of internal differences in response to contact with the Other, and above all, in response to conflict with the Other."[104]

In other words, the unifying idea of the nation emerged as the overarching element in a complex layering of individuals' experience of identity. As the nineteenth century progressed, social class became the critical element in this complexity and, as Arendt puts it, "[s]ocial status was decisive for the individual's participation in politics . . . except in cases of national emergency when he was expected to act only as a *national,* regardless of his class or party membership. . . ."[105]

The condition for imperialist expansion that led the bourgeoisie to begin the Great Game by fusing their economic interests with politics was their definition of a perpetual state of national emergency in which survival itself was at stake. It was a thinly disguised war between nations, sometimes overtly declared and fought, that exerted a remorseless pressure for everyone involved to "act only as a national." As a result, "the class system broke down and carried with it the whole fabric of visible and invisible threads which bound the people to the body politic."[106] Political life contracted as the space of society expanded to fill in the spaces of political differences with demands for conforming behavior from everybody in the name of winning the war for survival and domination.

It was, Arendt tells us, "[i]n this atmosphere of the breakdown of class society the psychology of the European mass man developed."[107] In the name of the nation's demand for universal conformity the experience of being an individual narrowed. The bourgeoisie, by seizing control of the power of the state and beginning the Great Game, had also ideologically reshaped how everyone understood who they were. Everyone was now expected to think of themselves as bourgeois enlistees in the nation's war for survival. How everyone was to fight seemed clear enough. Loyalty to the nation meant fighting the war for survival by living the bourgeois values in whose name the war was being fought. Everyone was to behave as the epitome of bourgeois individuality, pursuing their private interests of making money in whatever way they could, which would result in the greatest public good imaginable: The predestined survival of the fittest whose fruits would be delivered to every loyal citizen as the cure of his suffering from the tensions of the ills, which he defined as economic, that beset him.

In one sense it was not such a peculiar way to fight a war. Like soldiers have always done and continue to do, it is a matter of behaving correctly, while leaving the big picture for the generals to deal with in the secrecy of their war rooms. It is a matter of knowing and believing in the ideals for which one fights, then fighting and waiting to receive the fruits of one's loyalty. Yet there is this critical peculiarity: In thinking of themselves as fighting the good fight by epitomizing bourgeois values, people must think of themselves in the one way in which soldiers in a shooting war are forbidden; that is, as individuals, unconnected to each other, but supportive of competitive behavior that by pursuing private interests, yields the fruit for which the war is being fought. Put another way, everyone knows that they are part of something larger than themselves to which they must be loyal, but for the reason that they are individuals whose loyalty to this larger ideal can only be expressed through loyalty to themselves, they find themselves only able to experience their individuality in a peculiar way.

Arendt expresses this peculiarity in two interrelated ways: first, because ordinary citizens could only experience events produced by the Great Game as if they had been conjured up by stage magicians calling on mysterious processes for which nobody was responsible, they experienced what Arendt calls a "[s]elflessness in the sense that oneself does not matter, the feeling of being expendable. . . ."[108] The dissolution of its interest in public affairs left *mass man* with only the residue of a "passionate inclination toward the most abstract notions as guides for life" and, as Arendt acerbically notes, a "general contempt for even the most obvious rules of common sense."[109]

It is this loss of common sense that defines the second peculiarity in *mass man*'s experience of its individuality. Its passion to reduce the complex affairs of the world to Rhodes-like visions of annexing the stars, or Social Darwinist visions of realizing an evolutionary destiny, was correlative with annexing bourgeois rules for behaving in a complex world that, ironically, could only further alienate him from an interest in political affairs that controlled his life. We recognize these rules today. Nathan Glazer, reviewing Richard Epstein's book, *Simple Rules for a Complex World,* which recommends them, recognizes that they "lie at the basis of 17th and 18th century liberalism, and would have met full approval from John Locke, David Hume and Adam Smith . . ." and, we might add, Thomas Hobbes. "There are four basic 'simple rules.' The first is 'individual self ownership.'. . . One owns oneself, and the product of one's labor, and this is the best route to a productive society. The second rule, dealing with ownership of property, is 'first possession . . . you take what you can get'. . . which can be dignified under the term 'natural occupation.' The third is 'voluntary exchange' or the right of contract. The fourth 'deals with how to protect the things you have.' It 'forms the basis of the law of tort. . . . In its simplest and crudest form, the irreducible core of this body of law can be succinctly expressed: 'keep off.'"[110] As a result, *mass man,* suffering from a "selflessness" by living values that isolated him from others except in threateningly competitive ways, was loyal to a unified nation whose ideology alienated him from both the nation and himself.

To face a public space in which to achieve and protect a public identity whose primary measure was the accumulation of wealth that measured power, *mass men* were faced with a struggle to "keep their personalities intact if only because without them they could hardly expect to survive the competitive struggle for life."[111] They could only fall back on what they deemed to be a private space within which they could conduct their individuating struggle to coherently answer the question of who they were. The family became the only reality in which this could be accomplished. But here again, willing their "common sense" failed them. The experience of family as this private space existed only because they experienced themselves as selflessly expendable in the public space of society. The family became a refuge from which to escape the thinness of a public identity measured essentially by taking chances, which was the rule they knew only too well that governed making money. The family was experienced as the possibility of achieving what functioning in the public space not only denied, but made a mockery of: what Arendt has called "a mysterious irrational wholeness in man."[112] The bourgeoisie, Arendt tells us, becomes "the modern man of the masses, not in his exalted moments of collective excitement, but in the security (today one should say the insecurity) of his own private domain. He has driven the dichotomy of private and public functions, of family and occupation, so far that he can no longer find in his own person any connection between the two."[113]

We can get a better idea of what Arendt is alluding to if we read "family" as a metaphor for any private space in which the emotional life of individuals is at play. Arendt does not go far enough when she speaks of the private and public spaces as being "disconnected" in the "person" of individuals. As dichotomous as may be the emotionally sterile life of the public working-world and the emotion-filled life of the private world, from the vantage point of an individual's experience there is a crucial similarity. Experience of both fails to support the struggle for a coherent identity for *thinking, willing,* and *judging* beings that grounds their experience of being individuals.

When Arendt speaks of society demanding that individuals *behave* rather than *act,* she is not referring to demands for some mechanical-like motion that bypasses the use of the faculties of the mind, but rather to a way of using those faculties. These demands are complied with when *thinking* is concerned with calculating the self's position in the world rather than its meaning; when *willing* chooses available options rather than beginning new projects; when *judging* appraises the given meaning of things rather than being the entry into an incessant discourse with others over the meaning of whatever is being judged. What supports this "selfless" servility to the given meanings of the world, which assumes a commanding authority over *thinking, willing,* and *judging,* is the dream that conforming to that authority will realize the great good of unlocking the secret mysteries of the wholeness of the self. Hope for the same end supercharges the dreams behind the emotional life put into play in the private spaces of the world.

The condition of being a human being is to exist as an intention to display the meaning of what first—in the sense of primordially—appears to us. Here again, however, Arendt does not quite go far enough. We want more than to feel our emotions; we also want something to happen when we surrender our experience to them. Just as behaving in the public space feeds on dreams that subordinating passions to the calculated pursuit of interests will eventually cure us of the disorder of being absent to ourselves, the desire to surrender to our passions in the private spaces of our world feeds on the same curative dreams. Falling in love is undoubtedly a prime example. No age relies as much on love as a cure for the unwholesome self as does our own. The ancient tales of love as cautionary tales about the intimate relations between passion and death can almost be said to be sacrilegious at the end of the twentieth century—or at the very least, uneconomical.

Where only dreams about curing the self of the absence of itself matter in the spaces provided by society, the self's experience of struggling with the absence of itself can only be as fragile as the experience of being an individual. No matter how much we saturate the private and public spaces provided us with dreams of curing the self, all that can ever happen is that we display a meaning of how we appear to ourselves and to others whom we encounter in our world. In a world bereft of a space in which individuals can find support for bearing the burdensome condition of their individuality—i.e., of experiencing their beginning as having been inserted by chance into a story they never wrote and then to encounter, as Arendt tirelessly calls it, "a pluralistic world" in which they can never be the author of their own story—they become vulnerable to the terrors of existing at the mercy of lawless chance. When society expands in the name of "Nature or Divinity as the sources of authority for the *ius naturale* or the historically revealed commands of God [that] are supposed announce their authority in man himself,"[114] leaving no space that can support the actions of *thinking, willing,* and *judging* beings, then the experience of being an individual becomes vulnerable to the terrors of chance becoming the agency that rules the world. As Descartes and Hobbes showed in their different ways, a world of dreams offers only a thin resistance to existence under the rule of terror.

What Arendt clearly sees is that in such a world the very idea of the individual becomes the line across which the Nazis inexorably and dispassionately moved toward the horrors of the Final Solution.

~ 4 ~

Arendt's work confronts the uncanniness of the Final Solution—that which is strange and eerie that seems to defy being made familiar. In her essay, "Social Science Techniques and the Study of Concentration Camps," which was first published in *Jewish Social Studies* in 1950, she focuses on "the non-utilitarian character of the camps themselves—the senselessness of 'punishing' completely innocent people, the failure to keep them in a condition so that profitable work might be extorted from them, the superfluousness of frightening a completely subdued population. . . ."[115] She hazards the prediction that the function of the concentration as well as the extermination camps "in the larger terror apparatus to totalitarian regimes may very likely become that unexpected phenomenon, that stumbling block on the road toward the proper understanding of contemporary politics and society which must cause social scientists and historical scholars to reconsider their hitherto unquestioned and fundamental preconceptions regarding the course of the world and human behavior."[116]

With regard to the question of understanding the psychology of those who planned, administered, and staffed the camps, which Arendt does not explicitly take up in her essay although it haunts every page, her prediction cannot be said to have borne much fruit. Inquiring into their psychology typically centers on the question, *How could they have lived with what they were doing?* The question, rather than questioning "fundamental preconceptions," states the most fundamental preconception undergirding the idea for a science of human behavior: human behavior can be rendered understandable because individuals follow the formula of using means to realize an end. However different human behavior can be seen to be across time and place, it is governed by the means–end formula that operates outside of time and place. This formula does not exclude moral behavior, because it can be argued that behavior is always guided by some vision of "the good." Where moral life is violated, however egregiously, we must understand the conditions that cause individuals to pursue immoral ends. There has been no shortage of theoretical possibilities to account for such conditions, ranging from how individuals come to adopt the immoral ends they pursue, to how they can become blunted, anaesthetized, and deadened to the moral consequences of their behavior.

But the question that Arendt insists must be asked is not, *How could they live with what they were doing?*, but, *What was it they were doing?* Only if it is possible to identify the end that Nazi terror pursued can that question be suppressed, which risks understanding the meaning of an uncanny Nazi terror that makes "all our categories of thought and standards for judgment seem to explode in our hands the instant we try to apply them. . . ."[117] The question of what they were doing must be allowed to surface because, Arendt insists, it is impossible to identify the ends pursued by totalitarian terror: The "first characteristic of totalitarian terror [is] that it does not shrink but grows as the opposition is reduced. . . . Terror that is directed against neither suspects nor enemies of the regime can turn only to absolutely innocent people who have done nothing wrong and in the literal sense of the word do not know why they are being arrested, sent to concentration camps, or liquidated."[118] The pain inflicted in the camps was torturous, but we will never understand those who inflicted it if we think of them as torturers. Elaine Scarry has analyzed the meaning of torture in a way that shows us that to call them *torturers* would be a loose use of the word that misses the uncanniness of what they were doing.

Pain, Scarry tells us, is a terrible event "within the interior of [the] person's body . . . some deep subterranean fact, belonging to an invisible geography that however portentous, has no reality because it has not yet manifested itself on the visible surface of the earth."[119] The subject who suffers pain struggles to make it real by objectivizing it in a language shared by others, but knows that it is an unshareable experience because it resists language. The process of torture, Scarry tells us,

[I]n the very processes it uses to produce pain within the body of the prisoner . . . bestows visibility on the structure and enormity of what is usually private and incommunicable, contained within the boundaries of the sufferer's body. It then goes on to deny, to falsify, the reality of the very thing it has itself objectified by a perceptual shift which converts the vision of suffering into the wholly illusory, but to the torturer's and the regime they represent, wholly convincing spectacle of power. The physical pain is so incontestably real that it seems to confer its quality of incontestable reality on that power that has brought it into being. It is, of course, precisely because the reality of that power is so highly contestable, the regime so unstable, that torture is being used.[120]

What the torturer really wants is not information, which is usually already known or is trivial, but confession "to record and objectify the fact that intense pain is world destroying." Confession is betrayal of "oneself and all those aspects of the world—friend, family, country, cause—that the self is made up of."[121] For the victim, confession "is a way of saying, all is almost all gone now, there is almost nothing left now, even this voice, the sounds I am making, no longer form my words, but the words of another."[122] Confession is the victim's "extension out into the world . . ."[123] from the worldless and wordless pit of pain into which he had been placed by the torturer. But it is no longer his world into which the victim emerges. Scarry's analysis of torture points to its single purpose: to induce a pain that forces the victim to submit his very identity to a world that is totalized as the signs of power that belong solely to the regime that inflicts the pain. If torture is successful, the world of power into which the sufferer extends his pain, objectifying it to give it reality, confers on him a new identity in the name of the hope that it will be pain-free.

The pain induced in the Nazi camps was not designed to be like the pain induced by a torturer: an opaque cloud that obscures but does not erase the sights, sounds, and sensations that the victim receives from his own body and the surrounding world that tells him that he is still a human being facing the choice of confessing and emerging from his pain or of defiantly holding on to his pain-racked identity at the cost of his life. The victims of the camps, however, were already dead at their arrival—encountering, for instance, at the station at Auschwitz, as Primo Levi describes it, "everything silent as an aquarium"[124] with stone-faced guards interrogating in subdued voices. The prisoner's pain in the Nazi camps was like an afterthought inflicted on them as if they were, in Arendt's words, "like cattle, like matter, like things that had neither body nor soul, nor even a physiognomy upon which death could stamp its seal. It is in this monstrous equality without fraternity or humanity—an equality in which cats and dogs could have shared—

that we see, as though mirrored, the image of hell."[125] The pain induced in the camps was not designed to effect anything in its victims. The camps were designed to be "the laboratories in which the fundamental belief of totalitarianism that everything is possible is being verified."[126] In brief, they were designed to train those charged with inflicting pain and death in the practice of making real the terrifying image of hell.

Never before in the long history of the world had there been a government founding itself on a policy that its people create reality in the image of hell. Arendt, however, resists succumbing to the temptation of her own trope. Hell may be a region where no law rules to which the lawless are consigned, but she does not hesitate to call totalitarianism a "system of values . . . radically different from all others. . . ."[127] It does not value lawlessness: "[T]otalitarian rule . . . far from being 'lawless' . . . goes to the sources of authority from which positive laws received their ultimate legitimation, that far from being arbitrary it is more obedient to these suprahuman forces than any government ever was before. . . ."[128] It is also not the rule of one man who claims that he is the source of the law. Totalitarianism, "far from wielding its power in the interest of one man . . . is quite prepared to sacrifice everybody's vital immediate interests to the execution of what it assumes to be the law of History or the law of Nature."[129]

Its values are easily mistaken for lawless rule because while it values a world in which justice rules, it does not value the individual who will be justly ruled: "It applies the law directly to mankind without bothering with the behavior of men. . . . Its defiance of all, even its own positive laws implies that it believes it can do without any *consensus iuris* whatever, and still not resign itself to the tyrannical state of lawlessness. . . ."[130] It is able to avoid such resignation because it radically changes the relationship between human individuals and the law in a way that abolishes the very idea of the individual. The authority of laws rests on a tradition of possessing:

> [A] relative permanence as compared with the much more rapidly changing actions of men; and they derived this permanence from the eternal presence of their source of authority. Positive laws, therefore, are primarily designed to function as stabilizing factors for the ever changing movements of men. In the interpretation of totalitarianism, all

laws have become laws of movement. When the Nazis talked about the law of nature or when the Bolsheviks talk about the law of history, neither nature nor history is any longer the stabilizing source of authority for the actions of mortal men; they are movements in themselves.[131]

Totalitarian rule does not simply substitute a law whose nature is exhausted in the idea of movement for a law whose immovable nature is to govern movement. It defines the idea of an unmoving eternal presence of the law as nemesis. And with this idea as nemesis it posits the idea of the individual as someone whose conformity to the law stabilizes his identity as suffering from an illusion about suffering. Suffering is behaving toward an unmoving law as if one were moving like a puppet for a puppet master. Totalitarianism "can do without the *consensus iuris* because it promises to release the fulfillment of law from all action and will of man; and it promises justice on earth because it claims to make mankind itself the embodiment of the law."[132] There is no issue of governing on the basis of the people's consent nor, for that matter, is there an issue of the people withholding their consent. People embody the law and as such, their movement is the living presence of the law—they are its agent, not its servant.

What changes along with the meaning of the law and the dissolution of the idea of the individual is the meaning of terror: "In the body politic of totalitarian government, [the] place of positive laws is taken by total terror, which is designed to translate into reality the law of movement of history or nature."[133] Arendt sees that if we are to grasp the unique nature of totalitarianism, we must reverse our traditional understanding of terror: the traditional images of terror are the images of persons too paralyzed to move; but for totalitarianism, terror is the weapon of the law that calls men to action. But the call to action is not a call to act, which can only be directed toward individuals. Where individuals are only the embodiment of the law of movement, they are only motion-carrying terror that is its law: "Terror is the realization of the law of movement; its chief aim is to make it possible for the force of nature or of history to race freely through mankind, unhindered by any spontaneous human action."[134] It is possible to conceive of the law of movement as having an end in sight: terror releasing the world from itself by giving itself a form and a face—and who better than the infectious disease called the Jew? But terror can never end. To dominate the world means to be unable to stop using terror, for a world without Jews does not guarantee a world without disease.

It must be the performance of terror without end that takes the measure of men. The SS who ran the camps were the racially elite who were expected to display the character that made them the embodiment of the law of movement that was terror without end. Everyone else would either be followers, dominated subjects, or dead. But there could be no individuals, because the idea of the individual was a delirium in a world in which the law of movement reigned. This idea was the line that had to be crossed into a world that was ruled by terror without end:

> Terror as the execution of a law of movement whose ultimate goal is not the welfare of men or the interest of one man but the fabrication of mankind, eliminates individuals for the sake of the species, sacrifices the "parts" for the sake of the "whole." . . . It substitutes for the boundaries and channels of communication between individual men a band of iron which holds them so tightly together that it is as though their plurality had disappeared into One Man of gigantic dimensions.[135]

And of course for as long as a totalitarian government rules, for as long as the joy of discipline animates that One Man of gigantic dimensions, it must produce, without foreseeable end, monstrous evils.

~ **5** ~

We have been conditioned from the beginning of Western culture to insist that great evils demand great philosophies. But Arendt frustrates our expectations. She tells a conference of political theorists that she refuses to understand the meaning of the Final Solution as if it were an invitation to think toward a political philosophy of moral rules that can be translated into social policies: "What is the subject of our thought? Experience! Nothing else! And if we lose the ground of experience then we get into all kinds of theories. When the political theorist begins to build his systems he is also usually dealing with abstraction."[136]

Arendt turns our attention to something we need that is more banal than the abstractions of political theories: reconstituting a space in society that has been obliterated in the name of modernity, in which individuals can experience being individuals. Totalitarian rule, which banishes the idea of the free individual, points to this: A totalitarian government "does not just curtail liberties or abolish essential freedoms; nor does it, at least to our limited knowledge, succeed in eradicating the love of freedom from the hearts of man. It destroys the one essential prerequisite of all freedom which is simply the capacity of motion which cannot exist without space."[137]

Arendt's "love of freedom" is not just a slogan. As Kierkegaard taught us, we may exist as freedom in motion, but because our freedom is inescapable does not mean that it is like a treasure that compels being loved. For Arendt, the condition of being free is to be an individual whose motion begins with a meaning conferred on him in a story nobody authored in a world where nobody can ever claim to be the author of the story of their life. All of Arendt's work testifies that loving our freedom depends on more than feeling it in our heart. It is undeniable that feelings, in and of themselves, are powerful elements of our psychic life. Emotions, for Arendt, are inseparable from human intentions to constitute the meaning of what appears; but at the same time, if there are no meanings that are intended that are not emotionally charged, there are also no emotions that are not charged with meaning. Emotions can be unlocked by images and sounds that penetrate into that inner private world which we call, for lack of any other words, our heart and soul. But their meaning is unlocked only in the public world where others live:

> Unlike thoughts and ideas, feelings, passions and emotions can no more become part and parcel of the world of appearances than can our inner organs. What appears in the outside world in addition to physical signs is only what we make of them through the operation of thought. Every *show* of anger, as distinct from the anger I feel, already contains a reflection on it, and it is this reflection that gives the emotion the highly individualized form which is meaningful for all surface phenomena. To show one's anger is one form of self-presentation; I decide what is fit for appearance. In other words, the emotions I feel are no more *meant* to be shown in their unadulterated state than the inner organs by which we live.[138]

Emotions can, of course, be shown "by glance, gesture, inarticulate sound . . ." but doing so "is no different from the way the higher animal species communicate very similar emotions to each other as well as to men."[139] In other words, the condition of being human signifies that emotions are not meant to be shown as signs, but displayed as meanings.

Whatever it may be to feel free in our heart, insofar as it translates itself into something meaningful that we can speak about, "[w]e first become aware of freedom or its opposite in our intercourse with others, not in the intercourse with ourselves."[140] Freedom cannot be loved until it can be experienced as meaningful "in the plural realm of the 'many,'"[141] and it cannot be experienced as meaningful until it is lived in a space where individuals encounter each other as action and speech:

> Action and speech are so closely related because the primordial and specifically human act must also always answer the question asked of every newcomer: "Who are you?" The disclosure of "who somebody is" is implicit in the fact that speechless action somehow does not exist, or if it exists it is irrelevant; without speech action loses the actor, and the doer of deeds is possible only to the extent that he is at the same time the speaker of words, who identifies himself as the actor and announces what he is doing, what he has done, or what he intends to do. . . .[142]

To use words is not the sign of speaking as an individual. Speech is the medium by which we struggle to make sense of who we are as *thinking, willing,* and *judging* individuals to ourselves and others: *thinking* is the discourse we have with ourselves; *willing* is the promise we make to ourselves and others about who we will be in the future: *judging* is the endless discourse we enter into with others as we try to move from the meaning of what we are judging that is particular to ourselves, to a more general meaning.

Arendt heard Eichmann, in the Jerusalem courtroom, use words but never speak. He used words during the weeks of his long defense that were the same tired clichés, stock phrases, old saws he had used during the Nazi years, as if fifteen years had not passed at all since he had left behind in Europe literally mountains of corpses of the people he had transported to the camps. It is undeniably true that at many, perhaps even most, times people are no more likely to be reflexively conscious of the meaning of what they are doing when they do it than are animals.

But at some point, as the Greeks who invented tragedy insisted, people, unlike animals, must draw a line where the urgency to act ends, and retrieving the meaning of what was done that gives the actor a meaning, however terrible that meaning may be, begins. Eichmann knew nothing of that line, blindly moving in Jerusalem in the same steps he had taken as an SS officer, as if time had never passed—as if he were dead to being an individual who always has the possibility of beginning something new because he himself had entered the world as a new beginning. Eichmann was not an individual who could draw a line—he was the line crossed over that demolishes the very idea of an individual. Eichmann embodied the movement to create a world where nothing is impossible because the individual self is nothing.

For Arendt, evil, like terror, is ordinary, not in the sense of being encountered everywhere, but in the sense that when it is encountered it displays what is common to us all: the fragility from which we suffer our experience of being an individual for whom, because of an "already existing web of human relationships with its conflicting wills and intentions . . . action almost never achieves its purpose . . .," and for whom, "although everybody starts his own story, at least his own life story, nobody is the author or producer of it."[143] A society that denies people the space that supports the burden imposed by the experience of being an individual is not only a society that deals in a politics of brutality, but is sketching a line that was once crossed over by beginning to create a culture of terror. And where can we say that today we do not see practiced everywhere in the world, from the most to the least "advanced" societies, a terrible politics of brutality?

Notes

1. Ronald Beiner, "Interpretive Essay," in Hannah Arendt, *Lectures on Kant's Political Philosophy,* ed. Ronald Beiner (Chicago: University of Chicago Press, 1989), 89.

2. Arendt, *Lectures on Kant,* 15.

3. Arendt, *Lectures on Kant,* 10.

4. Arendt, *Lectures on Kant,* 15.

5. Arendt, *Lectures on Kant,* 42.

6. Arendt, *Lectures on Kant,* 43.

7. Arendt, *Lectures on Kant,* 54.

8. Dana R. Villa, *Arendt and Heidegger: The Fate of the Political* (Princeton, NJ: Princeton University Press, 1996), 70–71.

9. Hannah Arendt, *The Origins of Totalitarianism,* 3d ed. (New York: Harvest/HBJ, 1968), xv.

10. Hannah Arendt, *The Human Condition* (Chicago: University of Chicago Press, 1958), 45.

11. Arendt, *The Human Condition,* 23–24.

12. Arendt, *The Human Condition,* 24.

13. Arendt, *The Human Condition,* 28.

14. Arendt, *The Human Condition,* 25.

15. Arendt, *The Human Condition,* 30–31.

16. Arendt, *The Human Condition,* 40.

17. Arendt, *The Human Condition,* 45.

18. Arendt, *The Human Condition,* 41–42.

19. Arendt, *The Human Condition,* 42.

20. Arendt, *The Human Condition,* 273–74.

21. Arendt, *The Human Condition,* 275.

22. Arendt, *The Human Condition,* 274.

23. Ruth Morse, *Truth and Convention in the Middle Ages* (Cambridge, UK: Cambridge University Press, 1991), 1.

24. Morse, *Truth and Convention,* 3.

25. Carolly Erickson, *The Medieval Vision* (Oxford, UK: Oxford University Press, 1976), 7.

26. J. Huizinga, *The Waning of the Middle Ages* (Garden City, NY: Doubleday/Anchor, 1954), 10.

27. Arendt, *The Human Condition,* 4.

28. Hannah Arendt, *Between Past and Future,* expanded ed. (New York: Penguin Books, 1977), 39.

29. Piotr Hoffman, *Doubt, Time, Violence* (Chicago: University of Chicago Press, 1986), xi.

30. Arendt, *The Human Condition,* 278.

31. Arendt, *The Human Condition,* 38.

32. Arendt, *The Human Condition,* 69.

33. Karl Joachim Weintraub, *The Value of the Individual: Self and Circumstance in Autobiography* (Chicago: University of Chicago Press, 1978), xii–xiii.

34. Arendt, *The Human Condition,* 39.

35. Arendt, *The Human Condition,* 38.

36. Arendt, *The Human Condition,* 50.

37. Arendt, *The Human Condition,* 50.

38. Arendt, *The Human Condition,* 293.

39. Erving Goffman, *Stigma: Notes on the Management of Spoiled Identity* (Englewood Cliffs, NJ: Prentice-Hall, 1963), 1.

40. Goffman, *Stigma,* 135.

41. Arendt, *The Origins of Totalitarianism,* 91.

42. Arendt, *The Origins of Totalitarianism,* 54.

43. Arendt, *The Origins of Totalitarianism,* 54.

44. Arendt, *The Origins of Totalitarianism,* 11.

45. Arendt, *The Origins of Totalitarianism,* 13.

46. Conor Cruise O'Brien, "Nationalism and the French Revolution," in *The Permanent Revolution: The French Revolution and Its Legacy,* ed. Geoffrey Best (Chicago: University of Chicago Press, 1989), 9.

47. O'Brien, "Nationalism and the French Revolution," 18.

48. O'Brien, "Nationalism and the French Revolution," 19.

49. Geoff Eley and Ronald Grigor Suny, *Becoming National: A Reader* (New York: Oxford University Press, 1996), 139.

50. Arendt, *The Human Condition,* 39.

51. Liah Greenfield, "The Intellectual as Nationalist," *Civilization* 2, no. 2 (Mar.–Apr. 1995).

52. Peter Gay, *Education of the Senses,* vol. 1 of *The Bourgeois Experience* (Oxford, UK: Oxford University Press, 1984), 65.

53. O'Brien, "Nationalism and the French Revolution," 34.

54. Jacob Katz, *Exclusiveness and Tolerance: Studies in Jewish–Gentile Relations in Medieval and Modern Times* (Oxford, UK: Oxford University Press, 1961).

55. Katz, *Exclusiveness and Tolerance,* 3.

56. Arendt, *The Origins of Totalitarianism,* 8.

57. Katz, *Exclusiveness and Tolerance,* 3.

58. Arendt, *The Origins of Totalitarianism,* xi–xii.

59. Katz, *Exclusiveness and Tolerance,* 140.

60. Arendt, *The Origins of Totalitarianism,* 15.

61. Arendt, *The Origins of Totalitarianism,* 14.

62. Arendt, *The Origins of Totalitarianism,* 15.

63. Katz, *Exclusiveness and Tolerance,* 5.

64. Arendt, *The Origins of Totalitarianism,* 55.

65. Arendt, *The Origins of Totalitarianism,* 56.

66. Marion A. Kaplan, *The Making of the Jewish Middle Class* (Oxford, UK: Oxford University Press, 1991), viii.

67. Kaplan, *The Making of the Jewish Middle Class,* 3.

68. Kaplan, *The Making of the Jewish Middle Class,* 11.

69. Arendt, *The Origins of Totalitarianism,* 67.

70. Arendt, *The Origins of Totalitarianism,* 24.

71. Arendt, *The Origins of Totalitarianism,* 50–51.

72. Arendt, *The Origins of Totalitarianism,* 51.

73. Arendt, *The Origins of Totalitarianism,* 52.

74. Arendt, *The Origins of Totalitarianism,* 4.

75. Arendt, *The Origins of Totalitarianism,* 123.

76. Pierre Manent, *An Intellectual History of Liberalism,* tr. Rebecca Balinski (Princeton, NJ: Princeton University Press, 1994), 3.

77. Arendt, *The Origins of Totalitarianism,* xviii.

78. Edward Vose Gulick, *Europe's Classical Balance of Power* (Ithaca, NY: Cornell University Press, 1955), 10.

79. Gulick, *Europe's Classical Balance of Power,* 36.

80. H. L. Wesseling, *Divide and Rule: The Partition of Africa, 1880–1914,* tr. Arnold J. Pomerans (Westport, CT: Praeger, 1996), 80.

81. Arendt, *The Origins of Totalitarianism,* 125.

82. Arendt, *The Origins of Totalitarianism,* 136.

83. Arendt, *The Origins of Totalitarianism,* 137.

84. Eric Hobsbawm, *The Age of Extremes: A History of the World, 1914–1991* (New York: Pantheon Books, 1994), 29–30.

85. Hannah Arendt, *On Revolution* (New York: Viking, 1963), 54.

86. Arendt, *The Origins of Totalitarianism,* 139.

87. Arendt, *The Origins of Totalitarianism,* 139.

88. Arendt, *The Origins of Totalitarianism,* 140.

89. Arendt, *The Origins of Totalitarianism,* 140–41.

90. Albert O. Hirschman, *The Passions and the Interests: Political Arguments for Capitalism Before Its Triumph* (Princeton, NJ: Princeton University Press, 1977), 19.

91. Hirschman, *The Passions and the Interests,* 42.

92. Quoted in Arendt, *The Origins of Totalitarianism,* xviii.

93. Wesseling, *Divide and Rule,* 291.

94. Arendt, *The Origins of Totalitarianism,* 133–34.

95. Arendt, *The Origins of Totalitarianism,* 135.

96. Arendt, *The Origins of Totalitarianism,* 212.

97. Arendt, *The Origins of Totalitarianism,* 213.

98. Charles Taylor, "Wittgenstein, Empiricism, and the Question of the 'Inner'," in *Hermeneutics and Psychological Theory,* ed. Stanley B. Messer, Louis A. Sass, and Robert L. Woolfolk (New Brunswick, NJ: Rutgers University Press, 1988), 53.

99. Arendt, *The Origins of Totalitarianism,* xv.

100. Salvador Giner, *Mass Society* (New York: Academic, 1976), xii.

101. Arendt, *The Origins of Totalitarianism,* 314.

102. Linda Colley, *Britons: Forging the Nation 1707–1837* (New Haven, CT: Yale University Press, 1992), 1.

103. Colley, *Britons,* 6.

104. Colley, *Britons,* 6.

105. Arendt, *The Origins of Totalitarianism,* 314.

106. Arendt, *The Origins of Totalitarianism,* 314.

107. Arendt, *The Origins of Totalitarianism,* 315.

108. Arendt, *The Origins of Totalitarianism,* 315.

109. Arendt, *The Origins of Totalitarianism,* 316.

110. Nathan Glazer, review of *Simple Rules for a Complex World,* by Richard Epstein, *New York Times,* 16 July 1995.

111. Glazer, "Review."

112. Arendt, *The Origins of Totalitarianism,* 336.

113. Hannah Arendt, *Essays in Understanding: 1930–1945* (New York: Harcourt, Brace, 1994), 340.

114. Arendt, *Essays in Understanding,* 232.

115. Arendt, *Essays in Understanding,* 233.

116. Arendt, *Essays in Understanding,* 232.

117. Arendt, *Essays in Understanding,* 302.

118. Arendt, *Essays in Understanding,* 299.

119. Elaine Scarry, *The Body in Pain* (Oxford, UK: Oxford University Press, 1985), 3.

120. Scarry, *The Body in Pain,* 27.

121. Scarry, *The Body in Pain,* 29.

122. Scarry, *The Body in Pain,* 35.

123. Scarry, *The Body in Pain,* 33.

124. Pietro Frassica, ed., *Primo Levi as Witness: Proceedings of a Symposium Held at Princeton University April 30–May 2, 1989* (Fiesoli: Casalini, 1990), 8–9.

125. Arendt, *Essays in Understanding,* 198.

126. Arendt, *The Origins of Totalitarianism,* 437.

127. Arendt, *The Origins of Totalitarianism,* 460.

128. Arendt, *The Origins of Totalitarianism,* 461.

129. Arendt, *The Origins of Totalitarianism,* 461–62.

130. Arendt, *The Origins of Totalitarianism,* 462.

131. Arendt, *The Origins of Totalitarianism,* 463.

132. Arendt, *The Origins of Totalitarianism,* 462.

133. Arendt, *The Origins of Totalitarianism,* 464.

134. Arendt, *The Origins of Totalitarianism,* 465.

135. Arendt, *The Origins of Totalitarianism,* 466.

136. Hannah Arendt, "On Hannah Arendt," in *Hannah Arendt: The Recovery of the Public World,* ed. Melvyn A. Hill (New York: St. Martin's Press, 1979), 308.

137. Arendt, *The Origins of Totalitarianism,* 466.

138. Hannah Arendt, *The Life of the Mind,* vol. 1 (New York: Harcourt, Brace, Jovanovitch, 1978), 31–32.

139. Arendt, *The Life of the Mind,* vol. 1, 32.

140. Arendt, *Between Past and Future,* 148.

141. Arendt, *Between Past and Future,* 75.

142. Arendt, *The Human Condition,* 39–40.

143. Arendt, *The Human Condition,* 39–40.

Index

About the Author

Bernard J. Bergen is currently professor emeritus of psychiatry and sociology at Dartmouth Medical School and Dartmouth College, Hanover, New Hampshire. He received his B.A. from the City College of New York and his Ph.D. in social relations from Harvard University. He has been a consultant for several mental health agencies, as well as for the National Institutes of Mental Health, the National Endowment of the Humanities, and the Divisions of Mental Health in the states of Connecticut and New Hampshire. In addition to numerous articles and chapters in books, he has coedited *Issues and Problems in Social Psychiatry,* and coauthored *The Cold Fire: Alienation and the Myth of Culture* and *Medicine and the Management of Living: Taming the Last Great Beast.* His most recent book is *Illumination by Darkness: Freud and the Social Bond.*